FROM HEART INTO ART

FROM HEART INTO ART

Interviews with
Deaf and Hard of Hearing Artists
and Their Allies

RAYMOND LUCZAK

Handtype Press
Minneapolis, MN

ACKNOWLEDGMENTS

All interviews in this collection dated from 2003 to 2012 first appeared in *SIGNews*. (Exceptions, also dated in 2012, are Robert Arnold, Deborah M. Blumenson, Ph.D., Jennifer Dans-Willey, and Warren N. Churchill.) A few of the original *SIGNews* interviews included here have been streamlined for length. All interviews dated in 2014 are previously unpublished. The author gratefully acknowledges the pleasure of having worked with these editors at *SIGNews* over its nine years of existence: Jennifer Dans-Willey, Katie Prins, David Rosenbaum, and Adam Schafer. He appreciates the time spent at Phil Ferguson and Paul Ferreri's house which enabled him to restructure this book quite differently. The author remains indebted to John Lee Clark, Anthony Santos, and Tom Steele for their steadfast support over the years. Big thanks go to David Cummer for his editorial input.

COPYRIGHT

Handtype Press, LLC
PO Box 3941
Minneapolis, MN 55403-0941
handtype@gmail.com

ISBN: 978-1-941960-01-1
Library of Congress Control Number: 2014915360

A Handtype Press First Edition.

in memoriam

Chuck Baird, Artist
1947 – 2012

Phyllis Frelich, Actress
1944 – 2014

Betty G. Miller, Artist
1934 – 2012

Robert F. Panara, Poet
1920 – 2014

Robert J. Smithdas, Poet
1925 – 2014

CONTENTS

BLINK OF THE LENS

HAND-WROUGHT

FROM HEART INTO ART
Foreword

In this day and age, when human interactions seem so fragmented amidst a sea of tweets, status updates, and blog entries, the interview must seem like a solitary occupation. Two people meet to talk about something in common, usually a new book or an art gallery opening or a film; the interview is a conversation in which the people expect to be overheard and repeated in print and online. Sometimes it's shot on video and edited before it's released. But everyone seems to prefer sound-bites, often forgetting that these people have been reduced to only one element of their larger personalities and belief systems. Its context is usually lost.

You used to see interviews all the time. Now it feels like a lost art.

We need to "listen" to each other more closely than ever.

As a deaf person who'd joined the American Sign Language (ASL) community in the summer of 1984, I learned early on that it was usually important to find out the educational background of each deaf person I'd met. Knowing that would clue me immediately as to why that person signed in a particular way and held a set of certain attitudes toward the hearing community. Deaf people who'd grown up in hearing families often behaved differently from those who had deaf parents, and even more differently if they'd attended state residential schools for the deaf. Sometimes late-deafened people have a hard time learning ASL. Sometimes a hearing person could pick up on ASL fairly quickly and become interested in becoming a sign language interpreter. Sometimes a hearing Child of Deaf Adults (CODA) would have complicated feelings about growing up in an all-signing environment and overhearing strangers talk about their parents as if they were zoo animals, not realizing that the child was hearing. Sometimes a deaf person will proclaim herself as a Deaf person; the capitalization of the word "Deaf" indicates a non-medical view of deafness as a social, cultural and linguistic condition as opposed to a pathological condition requiring a surgical fix and otherwise. Sometimes a deaf person never learns sign language!

Deafness—much like art—is not a simple matter. It cannot be reduced to simple generalizations except for maybe one: The emotional price of misunderstanding by the hearing world is enormous, and the price of clarity by others who understand the pain of misunderstanding is always a bargain.

That's why some interviews start with one's educational and familial background. Their answers are often a shorthand code for us Deaf readers.

An useful term to use while discussing the Deaf experience is "audism." First invented by the researcher Tom Humphries in the 1970s, audism encompasses discrimination or stereotypes against deaf or hard of hearing people. For instance, some audists might assume that the cultural ways of hearing people are preferable or superior to those of the Deaf or signing culture, or that deaf people are somehow less capable than hearing people." This meaning has evolved from Dr. Humphries's initial definition of audism as "the notion that one is superior based on one's ability to hear or behave in the manner of one who hears."

Some Deaf artists find it useful to view their work as part of the larger narrative known as "Deafhood," a concept first coined by Paddy Ladd, a Deaf British researcher, in his book *Understanding Deaf Culture*. Largely inspired by the civil rights movement spearheaded by African-Americans in the 1960s, he sought lessons in Deaf people's history from which the Deaf community could benefit. Genie Gertz, a faculty member of the Deaf Studies Department at California State University, Northridge (CSUN), explains Deafhood succinctly in an online ASL video, of which an English translation follows: "Deafhood means a process, a journey for all Deaf people. It is not a measurement who is Deaf and who is not. It is a process of becoming the best Deaf human being one can become. There are two definitions: deafness and deafhood. Deafness is a term often determined by the medical field that focuses on abnormality, diagnosis, and handicap. It also focuses on looking at deaf people as individuals with hearing loss. On the other hand, deafhood is a process, not a state, which focuses on people's existential stances. Their existences strongly tie to normality, collectivism, and recognition of the shared beliefs and values. This is not about labeling one another, not about whether you are a big 'D' or a small 'd.' This is about all of us being deaf with full support of everyone's journey to reach Deafhood. That is to unite us all, not to divide us."

Yet a few artists in this collection consider themselves culturally Deaf and yet work with sound in their work. Identity has become far more elastic than I'd initially learned as a Deaf person wending my way through the Deaf community.

Other artists in this book talk about De'VIA (Deaf View/Image Art). Because not many Deaf artists were acknowledged in the hearing world, some felt that there needed to be a formal statement about Deaf art. In May 1989, nine Deaf people with a vested interest in art came up with "The De'VIA Manifesto":

> De'VIA represents Deaf artists and perceptions based on their Deaf experiences. It uses formal art elements with the intention of expressing innate cultural or physical Deaf experience. These experiences may include Deaf metaphors, Deaf perspectives, and Deaf insight in relationship with the environment (both the natural world and Deaf cultural environment), spiritual and everyday life.
>
> De'VIA can be identified by formal elements such as Deaf artists' possible tendency to use contrasting colors and values, intense colors, contrasting textures. It may also most often include a centralized focus, with exaggeration or emphasis on facial features, especially eyes, mouths, ears, and hands. Currently, Deaf artists tend to work in human scale with these exaggerations, and not exaggerate the space around these elements.
>
> There is a difference between Deaf artists and De'VIA. Deaf artists are those who use art in any form, media, or subject matter, and who are held to the same artistic standards as other artists. De'VIA is created when the artist intends to express their Deaf experience through visual art. De'VIA may also be created by deafened or hearing artists, if the intention is to create work that is born of their Deaf experience (a possible example would be a hearing child of Deaf parents). It is clearly possible for Deaf artists not to work in the area of De'VIA.
>
> While applied and decorative arts may also use the qualities of De'VIA (high contrast, centralized focus, exaggeration of specific features), this manifesto is specifically written to cover the traditional fields of visual fine arts (painting, sculpture, drawing, photography, printmaking) as well as alternative media when used as fine arts such as fiber arts, ceramics, neon, and collage.

Interestingly enough, a few Deaf artists in this collection have begun to wonder if De'VIA has to be all there is.

What does it mean to ask a stranger questions?

What do I hope to learn?

Why bother?

It wasn't the fact that I needed to turn in an interview for my "Spotlight On . . ." feature column to *SIGNews*, a national newspaper for the Deaf and signing communities, every month in order to get paid. It was the fact that I wanted to learn a little something about the world of arts. What have they learned that I should know?

It wasn't easy. It was sometimes difficult to find *anybody* interested in talking about her or his artwork. It was as if the assumption of promoting one's own work that hearing artists had taken for granted hadn't registered with many Deaf artists. I had to seek them out. Maybe it was a cultural effect, dictating that Deaf people weren't supposed to draw attention to themselves after a lifetime of living in the shadows of the hearing world. Sometimes in *SIGNews*, I begged repeatedly to switch the spotlight on someone new. Almost anyone would do!

In hindsight I am struck by the diversity and number of people I had the good fortune to interview. Many of them have already gone on to other things, other projects. Evolution is just another name for art.

As a journalist, I've always enjoyed asking questions because people are capable of surprising me with their answers. I like being surprised and learning something at the same time. I'd hate to use the word "educational" here, because that somehow diminishes the variety of responses, as if these people are supposed to be "educational" when they are above all artists. While many artists are actively engaged in the process of self-expression and, in some cases, collaboration with others, they usually don't try to "educate" others. This is particularly true among Deaf artists, I think, because as a Deaf person, I know what it means to educate others constantly.

But the real reason why I like asking questions is because I am constantly seeking answers to the eternal question of what it means to be a Deaf artist. After all, I'm a writer, filmmaker, playwright, and photographer myself. I know something about how their worlds operate. What it means to create is a question I attempt to answer every day.

This volume comprises roughly half of the previously published interviews I've conducted, usually via email, during my nine years at *SIGNews* before the newspaper was put on hiatus in April 2012. I've added 19 new ones since then for a total of 72 interviews. The ones chosen for inclusion here touch on what it means to be an artist affected by sign language and deafness in some fundamental ways, so that taken together, these interviews should convey something deeper about Deaf people and their hearing allies interacting in the arts.

One last thing: Why is this book called *From Heart into Art*? It's an English twist on the ASL sign for "expression," which shows the hands, once fisted as if from within the body, opening up like flowers as they are brought out into the open. Thus the ASL gloss for the book's title would be signed: "express-from-within art."

FACES LIT AFIRE

ANTOINE HUNTER

Choreographer and Dancer

As someone who's known a number of Deaf dancers over the years, I was naturally delighted to learn of Antoine Hunter. He lives in the Bay Area.

Raymond Luczak: What is the most annoying question you keep getting as a Deaf person?

Antoine Hunter: For me there haven't been any annoying questions; only funny ones like, "Can you feel the vibration?" Funny how hearing and Deaf people couldn't feel the vibration in the same way when horses, whales, bats, dogs, cats, birds, and other creatures can feel vibrations differently. These wonderful creatures can send and receive vibrations just like humans do; however, people don't often pay attention, that's all. They take it for granted. As a dancer, I have to hold still to feel the vibrations. If I move or jump, *nope*, I don't feel the vibrations. It's really hard to feel in ballet because of the soft music pitch, and I am always told to jump around.

Luczak: Could you tell us a little bit about your background?

Hunter: I was born Deaf. However, my right ear was hard of hearing, and many people have said that I talked funny and weird. Now that I'm fully Deaf, many say I talk great! I labeled myself Deaf at age six but people have forced me to say "hard of hearing" or "hearing impaired" because of how well I speak instead of how well I hear. My family is hearing, but I grew up with Deaf homeroom teachers. In most places where I was involved, I was always the only Deaf person or the only black person there.

Luczak: In terms of music, how well can you hear? What are some of your favorite songs?

Hunter: Before, with my hearing aids, I didn't have to turn up the volume high all the time. But without my hearing aids, you would find me putting my head and ear on the speaker while it is super loud. I demand strong bass.

I love the bandleader who played with James Brown. His name is Maceo Parker, and I love his song "Children's World" from his album *Roots Revisited*. It's about 11 minutes long, and it has enough pitch for every hearing level and vibration—it can be calm or crazy, and it can be slow or sped up and slowed again. No matter how you dance it, it will work. It means that no matter what I do and how I feel, it's correct, and I'm inspired!

There is a musician named Marcus Shelby. He is amazing and somehow I can feel what his music is saying. I don't know how or why, but maybe it's because we are black and we value community and family. I hope to perform his music with my own work one day. Someone once said, "I guess you hear what others don't pay attention to, and the music becomes clear." It's funny that they would say that because I'm Deaf!

Luczak: Are you able to hear enough melody, or do you rely just on the beat?

Hunter: Oftentimes, when I dance for someone, I don't stress about it. I just dance and hope I'm on the beat. But if it's really stretching, I have to be *so* on it and not easy to do. I'll take the music home and play it really loud and memorize the whole song. However, when I dance, oftentimes I don't need to worry about the music itself. I just remember the timing they want, and I make up my own music in my own head and spirit.

As for my own work, I don't like using songs that have lyrics in them. The timing is so strict with those songs, but instrumental music is not as strict. That why I like using world or jazz music. Its tempo and live reactions from the audience are really important to me so that whatever I feel, I'm in the moment of the music because I always "hear" new sounds as I find new vibrations within my movement.

Luczak: Were you always a dancer?

Hunter: No, I was a basketball player, a track star (800m), a theater actor, a teen bodybuilding champion, a conflict manager, a speaker/advocacy leader, and an avid churchgoer. I thought I was going to be the next George Washington Carver or a supermodel. When I was five years old, I knew I wanted to dance after seeing the Oakland Ballet, but Mom had no money. When I was in high school, I start focusing on dance classes. Which was funny because I'd taken class to get a date, but class was so hard so I forgot all about dating. Dance was a new way to communicate.

Luczak: How did you become a professional dancer?

Hunter: I took classes anywhere I could, and I found amazing mentors in Dawn James, a dance teacher at Skyline High School, and Reginald Ray-Savage, the director of Savage Jazz Dance Company, where I was trained for over ten years. I went to Cal Arts for college, and I still took classes anywhere I could. I always had my dance bag! I'd train in my living room, the shower, the swimming pool, the street. I did the same in New York, London, Cuba, and elsewhere. The best way to become a better dancer is to join as many dance companies as you can and risk it all to give your best to make the artist's vision come alive! Today I teach a lot of classes and after I finish teaching and when I'm done for the day, I still take classes to maintain when I have time. It can be hard because I'm so busy teaching in five locations and dancing with eight companies.

Honestly, I don't know when I became professional. It took me a long time to say that yes, I am a professional dancer. I was really hard on myself in many levels, and many would tell me that I am professional, but I say, Not yet.

Luczak: You're also a choreographer. How did that come about?

Hunter: I'm more proud of my work as choreographer than how well I dance. Most of the time while I was growing up, whoever hired me would ask me to dance and do whatever I want. I would make up something so good that the director or artist would ask me to teach the other dancers the choreography. That was fun but not easy, but I always found a way to teach them the dance I made and then suddenly I noticed I wouldn't be dancing the dance I made up. It happened often enough that I realize I was a choreographer! That's where I started to train harder because I wanted to be good enough for my own dances. However, it was a blessing because it made me a better teacher. I had a head start to be a teacher before I became a dancer. Many artists and directors would tell you that it is hard to get people to do what you want them to do, but I had a gift to be able to see what the artists and directors wanted and explain this to the dancers. I could also remember the entire dance without working on it for six months.

I work with all kinds of people—Deaf and hearing, male and female, disabled and able-bodied, gay and not gay, professional and non-professional. It's always funny that I have to tell hearing people that they should dance as if they're deaf, and then they can hear the music clearly without the distractions of someone's high heels clicking on the sidewalk or a baby crying so loud that you can hear it above the music. It's hard for hearing people to dance on the beat whereas I feel it because they oftentimes are too busy listening. Dancers who train or work with me for over six years are used to my approach. My goal with anyone I work with is to use dance like the X-men's powers to help each other. We have to learn our powers and decide to use it for light or darkness. If you don't learn about your power, you can hurt yourself or others who are near you. Art is alive in the passion of dance vibrating in someone's heart. It has the power to heal and even kill. I choose to use dance for healing as it saved my life when no one could understand me. Dance is my way to communicate anything I need to say. I hope to pass my wisdom on to others so they can learn to use the arts to bring them closer together for peace.

SHOSHANNAH STERN
Actress

In the last three decades, we've had a string of Deaf actresses making spectacular inroads in the TV industry. Shoshannah Stern is now tantalizing us with her new show *Threat Matrix*.

Raymond Luczak: Tell us about your first professional acting job.

Shoshannah Stern: I was on winter break from Gallaudet University during my senior year. On that break I felt as if I should just stop investing so much time thinking about acting since my graduation date was looming close. Two days after I made that decision I got a random email from the Warner Brothers Studio asking me to audition for a guest spot on their television show *Off Centre*. I was floored. I figured, What the heck, I'll just fly out to L.A. and get one actual-to-goodness audition experience under my belt, and then I will know if I can do this or not.

Luczak: What was your first audition experience like? Did you use an interpreter?

Stern: Not for the very first audition, but for the callback, yes. The audition was one in which a hearing person was speaking to a deaf person without any knowledge of sign language and the Deaf person was signing back, so it was appropriate not to have an interpreter.

Luczak: Hm. That's an interesting approach. How did you feel when you were told you got the part?

Stern: As if I were dreaming.

Luczak: What was it like to do *Off Centre*?

Stern: Amazing. I loved that I was able to start off with a character I had so much fun with and who I thought was a rare representation of a Deaf person.

Luczak: Was the script already Deaf-accurate, or did you have to work with the writer(s) and/or producer(s) to make your character more realistic as a Deaf person?

Stern: It was already realistic because my character was not about her deafness. I don't think having a character that is all about one thing would be interesting for anybody to watch, and it's not interesting to play either. There is no depth, no arc, no conflict. I'm personally sick of seeing Deaf characters pop up on television shows or film acting as if being Deaf colors their every move and personality trait. In fact, most of the time they have no personality. Deafness replaces that.

Luczak: Have you ever been offered parts that were just like that? As if you were supposed to be one big ear?

Stern: I've been lucky. I have auditioned for parts like that, but I've never gotten them. I will also never turn down a part because I feel I grow from every experience I have as an actor, and roles are few and far between.

Luczak: Let's move on to your next acting gig: *Providence*. Care to say anything about what you've learned from doing that show?

Stern: I thought I wasn't going to get the part because I was barely 21 at the time, and the character was supposed to be in her mid-thirties and a mother of a six-year-old deaf girl. But I loved being able to get into the psyche of a mother, getting in tune with the older, more maternal side of me.

Luczak: What about *ER*? Was it difficult to do that show?

Stern: I can honestly say that my audition for *ER* was my worst audition ever. I walked out of that audition and burst into laughter because I'd never screwed anything up as badly as I had in the *ER* audition.

Luczak: But you were chosen. They must've seen something in you.

Stern: Apparently, and the director was more verbal about his feelings about me as an actor than any other director I had prior to that, which was really interesting, because the impressions he said he got from me just from my ridiculously horrible audition turned out to be right on. I guess he must be one heck of a director because I wouldn't have booked myself.

Luczak: Let's move on to *The Division*. What was that like for you?

Stern: That was really the role of a lifetime. It's the role I'm most proud of, and the role I worked the hardest for. My character was raped practically on camera, and I was fortunate enough to never have felt anything like that, but it truly forced me to delve deeply for feelings of violation, for feelings of utter vulnerability and betrayal. It was also the role that led to *Threat Matrix*. I also worked with Marlee Matlin, and that was unbelievable.

Luczak: Let's talk a little bit about your acting experience prior to *Off-Centre*. You worked in theater, did you?

Stern: I've never really had professional theater experiences unless you can count two charity performances of Eve Ensler's *The Vagina Monologues*—one in D.C. and one in Sacramento by separate groups. I absolutely loved doing *The Vagina Monologues*. I hope I get to do it again soon; I want to do it as many times as I can. I loved that play because it truly changed me. I came into it truly hesitant about doing the monologue that [the director] Jane Norman assigned to me because it was graphic and I've always been rather private about such issues. But I ended up feeling so empowered about what I was doing—it was like, "I am woman, hear me roar!" Just such a deep, deep personal meaning doing something so intimate with other women and in front of people and having them truly, finally relate to issues they'd never considered before. Other than that I just acted in almost every school play [at California School for the Deaf, Fremont and Gallaudet] I could get my hands on! But I left Gallaudet one and a half semester shy of my degree. My father still berates me about that.

Luczak: Do you think that having a deaf family helped you along the way?

Stern: Absolutely. I think that's what made the difference. I was able to have full access to absolutely everything and anything. Family conversations were always important and I remember always asking so many questions and thinking critically at a young age. My parents always talked to me and my siblings like we were equals.

Luczak: How do they feel about your success as an actress?

Stern: They were a bit hesitant at first. I don't blame them—it is a tough business and if I had children, I wouldn't wish this life on them for anything. There is no stability whatsoever and it throws you in the public eye and holds you there. But my parents are my biggest fans. When they saw that I was serious about making the move to L.A. and was willing to invest everything I had in this, they were so very supportive and still continue to be, and they do visit me in Hollywood as much as they can. I'm blessed to have parents like them!

CHRISTINE SUN KIM
Non-Traditional Composer

Joseph Grigely, an esteemed artist in his own right, recommended that I get in touch with Christine Sun Kim as she was becoming known for her work in sound.

Raymond Luczak: When did you learn ASL? How did your parents feel about your Deafness? Where did you go to school?

Christine Sun Kim: My deaf sister and I grew up communicating in Signing Exact English (more Pidgin Signed English than SEE) and started using ASL in high school. After my undergraduate studies, I finally internalized it fully while I was in New York City, mainly because I lived with a couple of Deaf friends who were fluent in ASL.

My parents were overwhelmed with so much uncertainty when they had my sister and me, especially after having just immigrated to the States the year before I was born. Luckily, they sought support and options for us. They enrolled us at the Taft Elementary and University High School, both in Southern California. University High School had such a large number of deaf and hard of hearing students that it felt like a deaf institute within a high school at large. I earned my bachelor's degree from the Rochester Institute of Technology, my first master's degree from the School of Visual Arts in New York City, and my second master's from Bard College.

Luczak: What sort of things did you learn at Bard that helped you as an artist?

Kim: Oh God, it was one of the most intense and rewarding times in my life. I was a MFA candidate in the Music/Sound department under the Milton Avery Graduate School of the Arts. As a low residency program, it consists of three consecutive summers in the middle of the woods. The environment is fast-paced, a full schedule to the max, an unconventional approach to education, countless meetings with faculty of all different disciplines (writing, photography, film, sculpture, and painting), and nonstop interaction with colleagues—I only had two, sometimes three, interpreters with me on campus. I don't read lips nor speak with voice, so it was a bit troublesome at first. Later on, though, I managed to get past the breaking point in terms of interacting with non-signers. I'm much more comfortable with the way I communicate, and I seem to thrive on being in-between of everything and whatever and anything and . . . nothing. It took me a while to figure out how to stand on my own feet and approach practice without compromising my integrity. I received amazing support from experimental musicians such as Larry Polansky, Pauline Oliveros, Matana Roberts, Marina Rosenfeld, and many others. I came to realize that I'd instilled everyone else's notions of sound and silence into myself for all my life. Even to this day, I try to remind myself to find my own notions.

With that said, I've learned that you gotta build up your own social capital, especially that deafness still has its own stigma in today's society. You must double your time, your work, your effort, and so on. We need to just shut up and do it; be smart with your decisions (big or small); courtesy goes a long, long way; rejections mean nothing as long as your ideas are real; and finally, overcoming your fears will benefit you the most. I used to avoid writing in English and dealing with sound, but working with both has been rewarding.

Luczak: Prior to your explorations of sound, what was your relationship with music like? Or did you just not care at all?

Kim: When I was little, I never really quite questioned all those millions of sound norms I'd inhabited. I find it quite funny that I know these norms so well that, as my cousin described it, it's as if I lived in a different country and mindlessly followed their rules/customs.

Even though my degree is from the department of Music/Sound, I do not consider myself a musician despite the fact that I call myself a non-traditional composer. My main focus is on the conceptual aspect of sound work. Basically, I'm investigating and rationalizing my relationship with sound, spoken languages, music, speech, and many other things. I question things that I am curious about.

Luczak: What led you to use sound as a medium of exploration?

Kim: I was doing an artist residency in Berlin right after I obtained my first MFA in painting, but I never truly enjoyed the process of painting nor drawing. That depressed the shit out of me, but that's when I got my epiphany to approach sound in a way that I initially hadn't been entirely comfortable. After I got home from Berlin, I told my then deaf boyfriend that I might start going down the path of exploring sound, and he flat out told me that it was the dumbest thing he had ever heard. That's when I realized I could be onto something potentially compelling and controversial. And I was right: sound is the best way to communicate with society at large and has raised many ethical and complicating issues. The bottom line is that sound is a tool for my voice, and by voice, I mean my ideas and my self-existence and my presence.

It's been only a few years since I started working with sound. It's incredible to see that the more musicians I work with, the more "legit" my work becomes. This is a perfect example of social capital. The more legit, the greater my voice becomes.

Luczak: You've mentioned in a number of interviews this phrase: "ownership of sound." Why is this important to you? How would a hearing person "own" a sound for that matter? I mean, would you say that a signing Deaf American "own" ASL?

Kim: It's so easy to yield or compromise your process or decision to social norms, to people's perceptions of sound, without realizing it. It's essential that I maintain a degree of control (or entirely) with each project I do. When I was in Tokyo last year, I conducted 200 participants to vocalize the cue cards I made. I was guiding those people to become my voice, which was a direct reflection of my place in this world and how I needed to work with people in order to make my voice known. I was the one who produced the score, hence I was in full charge of sound, and it didn't matter whether I could feel or hear them. Recently, I did a performance where I played four sound files I recorded and edited previously, on my own. However, before I played them, I asked the audience not to tell me if they were distorted or not. Both are examples of ensuring that sound remains in my ownership, not theirs.

Hearing people already own sound but collectively. They can further own it by factoring out the general rules of sound and do it on a personal level, like being loud during a movie screening (a bad example, but you get the idea).

Deaf Americans do own ASL but sadly, only within the community. ASL still doesn't have a clear place in the eyes of law and education, so in that context, it's still out of our ownership.

Luczak: Even though many people in the hearing media seem fascinated by your interest in exploring sound, do you feel that you are seen more as a novelty than as an artist who happens to be Deaf and interested in exploring sound? What have the reactions from your Deaf friends and the Deaf community been like?

Kim: Definitely a novelty, but I believe my work is strong enough to stand on its own after novelty fades away. I feel incredibly lucky how many communities resonate with my work—musicians, painters, writers, activists, scholars, philosophers, scientists and inventors. At first I was worried that I would be pigeonholed permanently as a deaf and/or "disabled" artist (I use quotation marks because it's a highly problematic term), but with my leverage with all those crazy platforms, I've stopped worrying.

For the longest time, I never truly found my place as an artist in the Deaf community, but from the beginning, I have always had a tight group of deaf friends who were—and still are—completely supportive of my work. At first I was shy and uncertain about the new medium because it didn't feel . . . ethical as a deaf person. Certain deaf people seemed to be flabbergasted and suspicious about my work, and they even questioned my cultural identity. But as time goes on, I think they have grown to embrace what I do. It takes time and some open-mindedness.

JOHN KINSTLER

Stand-Up Comedian

When I first heard of John Kinstler becoming a stand-up comedian, I was a bit incredulous. I'd seen him play the baddie in my play *Snooty* years ago, and I haven't seen him since. I decided to catch up with him.

Raymond Luczak: How did you lose your hearing?

John Kinstler: I was born deaf with 80/90 dB loss in both ears. I have two sisters and no brothers. One of my sisters is deaf with the same loss. Our hearing loss is hereditary; a recessive trait on my mother's side of the family.

My family is very supportive in making sure that our deafness does not hinder us in doing things we want to do. I was raised orally and learned ASL at the age of 18. I first learned it when I attended the National Technical Institute for the Deaf (NTID) in 1984. Being involved in theater productions at NTID provided a smooth transition into ASL as I was able to learn ASL through rehearsals—what a fun way to learn ASL!

Luczak: How did you decide to become an actor? What kinds of shows have you done?

Kinstler: I think acting was something I always like to do even as a kid. I don't recall deciding that I want to be an actor; it just happened gradually as I was doing things I wanted to do and that was to entertain people. When I was little being mainstreamed in hearing schools, I used my humor to distract my peers from viewing me as a handicap and it paid off.

My first ASL performance was a musical, can you imagine that? I was not fluent in ASL at that time. I starred as Billy Bigelow in NTID's production of *Carousel*, which Jerome Cushman directed. I had to work with an ASL mentor to get my English out of my ASL! That was really challenging! I was King Duncan in *Macbeth*, which was a short role as he got killed early on in the show. I got demoted to stagehand after Duncan's death.

After graduating from NTID in 1989, I joined NTID's Sunshine Too Theater Company for three solid years. After Sunshine Too, I joined the National Theater of the Deaf touring company performing *Ophelia* for one year. I then joined the Cleveland Signstage Theatre (CST) production of *Children of a Lesser God* as Orin, and *The Glass Menagerie* as Tom Wingfield.

I have made three Entertainment/Educational videos for children, *Sign Songs*, which won the Parent's Choice Award in 1994, as well as *Sign ABCs* and *Sign 'N Songs*.

Luczak: What led you to do stand-up comedy?

Kinstler: I kept making people laugh by just telling them anecdotes and personal stories. I am a very observant person and I learned about the essence of being a person or character through theater. I guess it was an escape for me from being me. It was sort of like an out-of-body experience when I become a role. When life becomes dull, tragic or uncomfortable, I try to transcend from the situation and change it to a positive one the best way I can, whether by playing a character, signing songs or being a comedian.

Luczak: What have you learned from being a stand-up comedian so far?

Kinstler: I can give you a list.

• Know your audience(s) and relate to them. Find suitable material for the audience.

• If your memory isn't keen, keep a pen and pad handy with you all the times to jot down sketches.

• Remember why you are on stage, to make them laugh!

• Practice, practice, practice! Learn how to deliver your material (timing and punch line).

• Know your material well!

• Be true and don't be afraid to FAIL!

• Learn how to laugh at life and most importantly, yourself.

I hope to someday to compete on *Last Comic Standing*, and get recognized nationally for educating everyone about Deafness. I'd also like to create more videos focusing on comedy, music, and puppetry.

PATTY O.
Fashion Designer

It's always gratifying whenever I "hear" about other Deaf people pushing upward against the proverbial glass ceiling above us in so many industries. Fashion is one of the toughest fields to break into because—let's face it—fashion looks glamorous and easy. As fans of reality shows like *Project Runway* know, fashion is anything but easy. It's a lot of hard work that do not always get recognized, but Patty O., a Deaf fashion designer based in New York City, has managed to get a bit of buzz for her work. Retailers are taking notice.

Raymond Luczak: Tell us a bit about your educational background.

Patty O.: I began my education at the Clarke School for the Deaf, but I left for public school in Atlanta for three years, and then I returned to Clarke. I went to Lenior Rhyne College in North Carolina where I majored in Art Education and minored in small business. I received a M.F.A. in fashion design from the Savannah College of Art and Design in Savannah, Georgia. I was also a pattern-making major at Fashion Institute of Technology (FIT) in New York. I learned a great deal. Most importantly, I learned that there are countless fashion ideas, which led to my upcycling fashion business. [Unlike recycling, "upcycling" refers to using discarded materials to make higher-quality products.]

Luczak: When did you become aware of clothes as "fashion," rather than just what people wore to keep warm?

O.: I always thought about doing something with all the clothing that kept piling up in my closet, so I decided to create fashionable items out of them, such as sexy dresses or skirts out of sweaters and unused dresses. Then I decided to create my fashion company to spread my upcycling ideas.

Luczak: Tell us about your first show. What was it like?

O.: My first show for my thesis was awesome. I used the many different colors of animals and plants as the theme for the wardrobe. It came out better than I could imagine, with all the beautiful colors. I was very happy and knew then I wanted to be a fashion designer.

Luczak: Who are some of your favorite designers, and why?

O.: I do not have favorite fashion designers, but I appreciate Stella McCartney. She has been unfairly portrayed, but she influences me a lot. She makes clothes that do not come from animals and are Eco-friendly.

Luczak: It seems that you're into being "green." Can you tell us about that?

O.: I have always tried to support the green movement so I created my Web-based upcycling company, PattyO Designs, where we can stop wasting so much clothing by transforming them into different creations instead. That, I believe, is sustainable and green. I have received incredible press and hope that will lead to future success, where large retail companies buy my bags (I recently had an open-call at Macy's and Urban Outfitters is considering as well) and support the green movement.

Luczak: Where do you find your inspirations?

O.: Well, I love fashion and I care about the environment, therefore I figure the best way to combine the two is by upcycling clothing. Instead of throwing away your clothing for whatever reason, because they are old or they no longer fit, or if those sentimental clothing items that just hang in the closet, why not upcycle them into something new, hip, and wearable, while helping the environment by limiting waste? For example, upon learning how jeans were a major source of all wasted fabrics, I thought of a way to help the environment was to make a tote bag out of jeans and burlap with the trademarked "MADE FROM MY EX'S JEANS" printed on the side. But I really get inspired by interacting with my clients, who get really excited by the ideas we come up with all types of clothing items, where dresses become skirts, an Oxford shirt becomes an evening dress. Finally, the deaf community, especially my incredible friends, really inspire me with their never-ending support. I want to represent them well in my endeavor to break the stereotypes about deaf people, and show that we should never accept limitations and we can succeed in a hearing-dominated industry like fashion. That is my ultimate motivation.

ALEX CHU
Musician

Most people within the Deaf and signing communities are aware of Beethoven's Nightmare, a rock band consisting of Deaf musicians. I was most intrigued when I heard of The Deaf Band, a new group made up of Deaf musicians, so I emailed its founder, Alex Chu.

Raymond Luczak: How and when did you become deaf? What were your educational experiences like while growing up?

Alex Chu: I lost my hearing when I was five years old from unknown causes. Nobody really noticed until the next day when my schoolteacher realized I wasn't responding to her whenever she called out my name. Next thing I know I'm placed in a classroom full of deaf students.

My educational experience was awesome! I was pretty much mainstreamed throughout my school years, and eventually graduated from New Jersey School for the Deaf. In college I studied to become a Network Administrator and at home taught myself all about web development. In the end, I decided web development was what I wanted to do, and still to this day it's what I do.

Luczak: If you were deaf at a young age, what led you to music? And what types of music did you listen to?

Chu: My mother used to turn on the radio and play music all the time in the house. Back then artists like Lionel Richie, Cyndi Lauper, and Boy George were popular so I'd listen to them although I didn't get every word they sang. I remember thinking the ending of Cyndi Lauper's "Time After Time" music video was cool because sign language was used.

Around that time it was when I met Dwayne Holliday that I discovered heavy metal like Metallica, Iron Maiden, and W.A.S.P. He'd wear these black heavy metal band T-shirts in school, and curiosity got the best of me.

Luczak: What were some of your experiences in the Deaf community when you shared your feelings about music?

Chu: Honestly, not many were interested in music, which was understandable, but whenever I'd meet someone who did he/she was my best friend (laughs). It was just rare finding deaf friends who shared the same interest, and it still is! However, I'm fortunate to have found a few who are now part of The Deaf Band.

Luczak: What led you to start up a new band? Why the name?

Chu: The notion of jamming together with other deaf musicians is fun! I've always wanted to do that but the deaf musicians that I knew lived so far away, and meeting to jam was impossible. One day I posted an ad on DeafNYC asking for local deaf musicians who'd like to form a band, and within the next few days I started getting replies!

We wanted a name that's short and sweet, and easy to remember, but at the same time described what we are and what we do. That's when The Deaf Band was born. Luckily, the domain name was available, and we now have a web site.

Luczak: What are you hoping to accomplish with your band in the near future?

Chu: Right now we're working on some songs together and have an album complete by next year. Some of these songs are about our Deaf experiences. We're also working with a Deaf filmmaker who would be doing an ASL music video for us that will be released online. In the meantime, we try to meet up for jam sessions and have fun.

OLEG GOLOVUSHKIN
Theater Director and Filmmaker

When I first heard about Oleg Golovushkin's work as a filmmaker, I was intrigued and asked to meet with him even though I didn't know Russian Sign Language (RSL). Here was a deaf Russian filmmaker living in New York City, and at the time, he was working with Marina Fantsheyn, a Deaf multi-lingual Russian woman (she knew ASL, Russian Sign Language, English, and Russian), to get his *TOYS Theater* show on the road. Marina interpreted our first meeting, and it was absolutely fascinating to see how my ASL was translated into RSL. We rarely saw each other since then as he was busy touring his show with his troupe of four deaf Russian actors—all of whom are masters of pantomime and humor onstage—all over the United States.

Raymond Luczak: What was it like to be a deaf person in the communist Russia?

Oleg Golovushkin: For deaf people in communist Russia, it meant we were guaranteed work like other citizens, but our choices of trade were very much limited. We do not always manage to find the jobs that we wanted. Hearing supervisors could ask the government and set up companies to hire us deaf people, but part of our money earned by such enterprises went toward the building of Cultural Centers, apartment buildings, and houses for the deaf community. Nearly all large cities in Russia had deaf organizations that were funded in part by deaf workers. Deaf people could expect free health services, a small state pension that was paid during their entire lifetime regardless of salary, free public transit services, and a 50% discount on all trains within the limits of Soviet Union. However, the ideology of communism required that we all be very close to the state and be limited to the information permitted by the communist ideology. It was impossible for a deaf person to visit outside Russia, and of course, individualism and independence were not encouraged as total collectivism was practiced. The state told us how to live, think, and run our lives.

Many people have asked me whether it was better to live in communist Russia or post-communist Russia. I have an analogy that may help clarify my feelings on this question. Under the communist system, a bird in a cage is fed with water, meals, and everything, but the bird must stay inside its cage. In the post-communist world, the bird is freed of its cage, but the bird must fend for itself while looking for food and water. Is the bird ready for a new life? Certainly the older generation brought up by the communist ideology does not feel as capable as those of the younger generation.

Personally, in spite of the problems posed by the post-communist world, I find that democracy has opened up new opportunities and prospects. I am glad of this, and I do not regret the change.

Luczak: Did deaf artists get support from the state?

Golovushkin: In communist Russia, artists got support from the state and deaf cultural organizations as long as their talents did not contradict the communist ideology. But now, in modern Russia, priorities have changed as the focus is no longer on creativity, but on survival.

Luczak: What was it like for the Russian deaf community when Russia was no longer communist?

Golovushkin: During the communist years, deaf cultural organizations followed the ideology of the state, and as such, they were very stable as the money from the deaf workers came in regularly. The money that came in depended on the amount of work that our enterprises attracted from the government; more money often came in from enterprises that had large orders and state factories required to meet these orders. These monies were used toward the development of organizations to help meet the cultural, social, and habitation needs of deaf workers as well as new construction required to house them. But after the disintegration of the communist system, these state factories ceased getting such large orders and therefore had to lay off people. Generally, deaf people were laid off first. Deaf workers now had to fight for—and to keep—their jobs. They also had to study how to demand and ask for money from the state in order to give opportunities for themselves and their community.

Luczak: What prompted you to set up the Russian Deaf Professional Theater in 1985?

Golovushkin: The St. Petersburg Cultural Center of Deaf Persons offered many courses in painting, drawing, and acting, but I saw that many deaf people were most interested in having a theater focused on pantomime. Over the years their numbers dwindled down to these four performers [Alexander Filimonov, Vasily Solonitsky, Lyudmila Romanovskaja, and Ilya Goltsov], who were indeed the most committed to the craft of pantomime. They wanted to come up with unusual skits that would awe their audiences, and so when they came up with the idea of a red light following a short fat man with a remote control, they knew they had something. Unfortunately, we had to close the theater in 1992 due to a lack of economic and professional prospects. We thought it would be closed forever.

Luczak: What was going on at the time that made you decide to do this?

Golovushkin: In 1994, I was invited to work as Executive Director of the St.-Petersburg Cultural Center of Deaf Persons. It was entirely up to me to help stimulate the creativity of deaf actors, artists, and poets. First I decided to revive what had already been done by deaf directors who had been doing songs and pantomimes before these positions were taken over by hearing people. I assembled the four actors of *TOYS Theater* and asked them to return to the stage and made it my personal responsibility. I knew they had great talent, and I wanted the world to see them.

Luczak: What were your stage/theater experience like prior to setting up *TOYS*?

Golovushkin: Before I began working on *TOYS Theater*, I had gone to university where I studied law, but after I graduated, I chose to work as a professional photographer. I was asked to teach photography and interacted with some faculty members who taught cinema. I decided to write a script for a two-minute film about deaf people. The short went on to win quite a few awards from various international film festivals. I could've continued working in film, but I chose to do art photography as it gave me more latitude and independence in my creativity. I helped run a business where I hired deaf people to do interior design orders. When I worked as Executive Director of the St.-Petersburg Cultural Center of Deaf Persons, I had to deal with the politics and the finances of the organizations in addition to motivating deaf artists to create.

Luczak: Were there other deaf theater companies that you saw who inspired you to do similar things but in your own way?

Golovushkin: Yes, I was very strongly affected by Vyacheslav Polunin's approach to creativity and acting, as well as Charlie Chaplin's skills in his films. I had a strong desire to make my work accessible to all without needing to rely on language. I tried to do the same with my short film *Cacus*, where I felt that the expressions and actions of my actors made everything accessible to all.

Luczak: You were interested in photography and filmmaking for a long time. Do you feel that your fascination with this process influenced you as a stage director? How do you work with your actors?

Golovushkin: Any experience has application in a life, whether it be legal, business, creative, or administrative; all are vital. Taken all together, they have given me what I possess now. And these experiences have helped me to achieve the results I did with *TOYS*. Of course, we are not content to let the show stay the same; we are constantly improving it through improvisation and new skits. After each show we always discuss details of our execution and where we can improve for next time. Constructive criticism helps us. My goal is to create ideal conditions not only for their successful performance but also to give them a stability in life itself. Because we truly love our audiences, and we all perform out of love.

Luczak: You've been staying in this country since 2000. Do you have some general observations on America? The American signing community? What do you wish that the American deaf community would get from the Russian deaf community?

Golovushkin: Yes, that's a very interesting and good question. America in terms of size is big as Russia; Americans are just the same as Russians. But historically America is different. Here, I feel that democracy is truly built upon the respect for human rights. The deaf person in America has incomparably more rights than the deaf Russian. When I was in America for the first time, I was very much surprised that so many hearing people knew sign language, and that ASL was considered an "official" language, because in Russia, RSL is not even considered. I feel strongly that this kind of experience and respect would benefit all Russians. Americans, I find, are a very kind and welcoming people.

Luczak: Have you been learning ASL, or do you still find it difficult to learn? If it's difficult, why is it hard for you to learn? Is it because RSL is so deeply a part of you?

Golovushkin: At present I'm not too bad with ASL, but with my own actors, we use RSL. For the last three years in the United States, I have met a lot of theater colleagues and a lot of interesting people. If I didn't know ASL, I would've lost out on so much. Being in America this long meant that if I didn't take the time to learn ASL, I would be showing myself disrespect by missing out on opportunities to learn more about the rich and interesting culture and lives of deaf Americans.

SHANNY MOW
Playwright

As a deaf playwright learning his craft, I kept coming across the name of "Shanny Mow." I knew he had been involved with both the Fairmount Theatre of the Deaf (now rechristened the Cleveland SignStage Theatre) and the National Theatre of the Deaf (NTD). Naturally, I wanted to know more about Shanny.

Raymond Luczak: Where did you grow up? What was your family like?

Shanny Mow: I was born in Stockton, California; my folks had immigrated from South China in the mid-30s. In Chinese parlance, I was number four of five sons; I had no sister. Cantonese was spoken at home; my mother didn't know English. All my brothers graduated from college—an architect, two dentists, a teacher (me), and a lab technician. I am the only one deaf.

I went into coma from spinal meningitis at age of five, and woke up with no memory of having ever heard. I attended California School for the Deaf in Berkeley; while there, I started to learn ASL and English at the same time at six years old. I graduated from CSD as valedictorian in 1956; a B.S. in Education from Gallaudet University in 1961; and a M.A. from California State University in Educational Administration (Leadership Training Program) in 1977. In between, I undertook graduate studies at San Francisco State (special ed), University of Tennessee (media) and University of California (linguistics).

Luczak: How did you end up in theater? And NTD?

Mow: I was teaching at Diamondhead School for the Deaf in Honolulu when I got together with Bernard Bragg whom I knew from CSD. He was on the last leg of his goodwill around-the-world trip on deaf theater. He encouraged me to send a script for NTD's Deaf Playwright Conference. I did and was invited to attend the five-week program on a Ford Foundation scholarship. Two other writers invited were Ruth Brown and Steve Baldwin. We met for seminars on playwriting in the mornings and retreated to our rooms to write in the afternoons. At the conclusion of Conference, I was invited to join the NTD company as an actor. I had no previous training as an actor let alone any in-depth knowledge of theater. I like to believe that I was invited as a part of David's grand design to have full-scale NTD productions written and directed by deaf persons together.

It happened the following year (1980) when Ed Waterstreet and I did *The Iliad, Play by Play*.

Luczak: Has ASL affected your personal and professional development as an artist?

Mow: Let's say my love of the English language is central to my professional development. Perhaps personal, too as reading is an important part of my life. Since most of my playmates at CSD spoke in ASL, I feel equally at home with ASL, but I don't think in this language when I write. However, without my being conscious about it, I'll write what will work in ASL. It is exciting to be able to produce clever English that will work in ASL, too. Actually, language is no more than a tool. You can write eloquent English or sign eloquent ASL and still have nothing to say.

I would write a sentence, a paragraph, a scene again and again until I feel the flow of words, ideas and action is right. I may rewrite the darn thing twenty times. Writing is rewriting. Writing is organizing. Playwrighting is writing dialogue. Dialogue must carry forward the movement in the story, inciting actors to action. Finally, writing is discipline. I write in the morning, do errands and whatever I need to do in the afternoon. If I get on a roll, I may write all day.

DAN McDOUGALL
ASL Theater Interpreter

When a friend sent me to the TerpTheatre's web site, I was immediately impressed by their clearly-defined mission of providing theatrical interpreting in the Detroit area. I decided to ask its founder, Dan McDougall, a few questions.

Raymond Luczak: What prompted your interest in ASL?

Dan McDougall: I was really into theater when I was in high school, and heard about this summer stock production of *Runaways*. I didn't know anything about it—except that the show was about runaway kids; and that I'd be working with older kids all summer. When I checked out the script, all the musical numbers had this note in the margin: "Hubbell sings." All over the place: "Hubbell sings" … "Hubbell sings." I figured that was what I wanted—a chance to show off my singing voice! (For the record, my singing voice isn't much to brag about!)

I went through the whole audition—acting, dancing, and singing my heart out. I lobbied the director, telling him I really wanted Hubbell's character. In truth, I don't think I really read the whole play. I was just excited about singing in just about every number!

I got the part. The director congratulated me: "Now, go learn sign language." My jaw dropped. It turned out that I misread the script: "Hubbell signs." Hubbell was Deaf, and I wasn't going to sing anything! Oh, I really messed up that show. I mean, I got out the book *The Joy of Signing*, and did a sign-for-word translation of all my lines and all the lines from most of the show. The show has an interpreter written in—but there wasn't one. So they had me "interpret" each song. Of course, it was a train wreck. Lots of Signed English stuff. I'm a big ASL advocate; but even real Sign English pros would've thrown me back into the water.

Luczak: What did you learn from your first theatrical interpreting gig?

McDougall: Kim Willett, whom I had known while studying for a B.A. in Sign Language Studies at Madonna University, invited me to interpret with her for Wild Swan Theater. They produce professional theater for children and include interpreters in every performance. They were pretty new at the time, but totally committed to accessibility. Kim had worked onstage with them in a previous show requiring only one interpreter. But *Alice in Wonderland* needed two.

At Wild Swan, interpreters are blocked into the scenes as they are developed. Because they have a collaborative ensemble approach, this gave us loads of experience developing the strategy for a scene. We interpreted every performance and had the chance to do as many as 60 performances of a given production. I ended up doing a lot of physical stuff, including Russian folk dancing. All this moving around the stage gave us a lot of confidence in movement while being coached on the acting side of things. We rehearsed with mirrors, which enabled us to refine the physicality of our characters just enough but not so to take away the focus from the actor. That training really helped establish the TerpTheatre's shadowing style.

Luczak: How did TerpTheatre start?

McDougall: After Kim and I worked with Wild Swan on my first show, I was also working at the Toledo Repertory Theater. Then we were at The Attic in Detroit. All of this was under the guidance of our mentors Mary Higgins and John Ray, who were doing amazing work at the Michigan Opera Theater.

When Kim and I began working with Shelly Tocco, we began to formalize our approach more, and I developed the TerpTheatre's web site. The site was designed as an educational tool for our theater clients; but the name, TerpTheatre, stuck. Shelly and I set up TerpTheatre just as we began providing workshops.

Luczak: How much time does TerpTheatre spend on translating a script?

McDougall: Our general guideline is that we want the script four to six weeks before our performance—naturally, this doesn't always happen. We have a list of tactics that help us divide characters on stage, while taking into account their movement, furniture, and lighting. Between this analysis and seeing the show, we assign roles to the two interpreters. Shadowed shows require more of our time onstage during rehearsal than shows where we're placed off to the side. We identify any language issues and all parts of the script that require us to sign in unison. The rest of the process balances individual rehearsal, working together, and working onstage.

Our approach is to support the two onstage interpreters with a third TerpTheatre staff member. That person serves many purposes: understudy, language consultant, blocking strategist, costume consultant, and house interpreter on the night of performances. This third person is vital, almost as a producer of sorts. All new interpreters who work for us start as interns, working with the third interpreter, so everyone is always on the same page and working with the same vision in mind.

Probably the most controversial part of TerpTheatre is that we don't regularly utilize Deaf signmasters. We have, on occasion, depending on availability of signmasters. We've had few local folks that we have identified with the interest, availability, and background; but we're hoping to find ways to include more Deaf signmasters as we keep growing.

WARREN N. CHURCHILL
Music Teacher

Some years ago when I lived in New York, I met Warren Churchill. I was impressed by the fact that even though he had a hearing problem, he still taught music to high school students.

Raymond Luczak: Can you give us a quick rundown on your background?

Warren N. Churchill: Well, I'm an only child. I was born near Boston, and my mother raised me on her own. During the early 1970s the economy was in a tailspin, and we ended up living with my grandparents in upstate New York for several years. During this time, I attended a regular public elementary school in a small rural town. Years later, when things got better, we moved across the Hudson River to Catskill, where I attended the local junior/senior high school. Other than sitting in the front row in my classes, no special accommodations were made for my hearing issue. I just did the best that I possibly could.

Luczak: Which came first, your hearing loss or your interest in music?

Churchill: I had spinal meningitis at the age of two and a half. But I'm pretty sure that music must have appealed to me as a toddler. I have old reel-to-reel tapes of me singing recognizable nursery rhymes and such.

Luczak: How did you become interested in music? What instruments did you learn to play?

Churchill: My mother had a huge influence on my interest in music. She was a soloist in her high school choir, and she played oboe and saxophone as well. I have fond memories of her singing to me as a child during our long car trips to visit my grandparents. As an only child, I spent many hours singing along with my record collection. I recall a school assembly during second grade where two teenagers sang a duet that moved me to tears. That was a formative moment. Years later, I joined the school choir and learned to play the clarinet in the school band. My closest friends were quite musical as well. Over the years, I've learned to play just about everything—piano, guitar, saxophone, bassoon, and flute— even bagpipes!

Luczak: What does music mean to you? Do you have particular musicians that you "worship"?

Churchill: I prefer to keep an open mind toward the many different forms of music making out there. I'm not comfortable with the idea of "worshiping" any particular musician or genre of music. However, I do admire singers like Whitney Houston, Eva Cassidy, and Audra McDonald. Similarly, instrumentalists Richard Stoltzman (clarinet) and James Galway (flute) are quite amazing as well. What I appreciate about all these musicians is their ability to communicate emotionally through a seemingly effortless mastery of their voice or instrument. By the same token, when I've watched Bernard Bragg in performance, I can't help but feel that I'm witnessing a similar sort of virtuosic visual "music" through Deaf poetry. I'm open to the idea that what we call music can be so much more than just sound.

Luczak: Please tell us a bit more about the type of hearing loss you have, and how it's affected your appreciation of music.

Churchill: I'm "stone deaf" on my left side, as they say. My right ear has what audiologists call a "cookie bite" hearing loss pattern. This means that I can hear well in low and very high frequencies. However, I have about a 70 dB loss in the middle (speech reception) frequencies. Of course, this makes it difficult to understand people at times. I also have trouble hearing certain electronic sounds, police sirens, and public address systems. Being able to hear the highest overtones of flutes, violins, and oboes creates the illusion that I'm hearing everything musically, although I know that's not the case. I also tend to focus more on bass lines and chord progressions, rather than the lyrics of songs.

Luczak: Did you have schooling in music specifically?

Churchill: I attended the Crane School of Music at SUNY Potsdam, where I graduated with a Bachelor of Music degree. I majored in music education and classical singing. It was a very rigorous program that required full-time dedication. After teaching for a decade, I went on to earn my M.A. and Ed.M. degrees from the music program at Teachers College, Columbia University. These days I'm still there, working toward finishing my doctorate.

Luczak: How did you become a music teacher? Was your hearing loss ever an issue with your students?

Churchill: I went through the usual certification process that most teachers go through in New York State. In my first student teaching assignment, I taught high school band. It went well, although at times, it was difficult to hear students speaking from so far away as I stood on a conducting podium.

During my second student teaching assignment, I taught elementary general music in a classroom. I found this to be much more enjoyable as I could move around more easily among my students to hear them better.

These days I teach at a very nice public school in Manhattan. I'm very open about my hearing issues with my 550 young students. They're generally very helpful and understanding. In fact, several of my hearing music students actually attended the preschool program at Manhattan's "47"—The ASL and English

Lower School. They know how to fingerspell and some basic signs, which has been useful in the music room at times.

Luczak: It's my understanding that you've done quite a bit of research on music and deafness. What were some of the more surprising things you've learned along the way?

Churchill: Initially I thought it would be hard to find any "evidence" of music in Deaf settings. As I've ventured out into the Deaf world, I was surprised to find that music is usually happening at Deaf events in some way or another. I was particularly impressed with the different kinds of music featured during the opening ceremonies of the 2010 Las Vegas Deaf Expo.

I guess what surprises me even more these days is that when I discuss my research-in-progress with my hearing musician colleagues, they seem to be amazed that Deaf musicians even exist. It's as if I were describing a unicorn or leprechaun sighting. But I don't think Beethoven's Nightmare, Signmark, or T. L. Forsberg should come as a complete surprise to music educators in this day and age. I hope by spreading the word, some perceptions can be changed a bit.

Luczak: Did you feel that Deaf culture has a lot to teach hearing people about communication, or do you think that's a bit overrated? Why did you learn ASL if you seem to be able to function enough with your residual hearing?

Churchill: Although I grew up in the hearing world, I've always wanted to learn sign language. Back in 1980, my mother signed me up for a "sign language" class offered by the local YMCA in Catskill. I learned to fingerspell, and I also learned a little bit of what I now recognize as Signed Exact English (SEE).

In 2004, I took a class with Dr. Rusty Rosen at Teachers College that "opened my eyes" to Deaf culture for the first time. Up to that point, I had always thought of myself as being "hearing-impaired," and this graduate course invited me to question things a bit. Thereafter, I started taking ASL classes, while gradually working up the nerve to attend Deaf events. I eventually settled into a routine of weekly tutoring sessions with an incredible ASL teacher and performer, David Rivera. He has been a tremendous help to me.

Does Deaf culture have anything to teach people about communication? Absolutely! But I think it's something that hearing people have to actively seek out and be receptive to. Speaking for myself, I felt an exhilarating sense of accomplishment when I realized that I was finally able to take in a story visually—to be fully absorbed in seeing language. As I continue to work on my ASL and attend Deaf events, it seems that I'm moving beyond the "hearing-impaired" identity I once grudgingly resigned myself to.

Luczak: You performed in The Deaf Band. What was that like for you?

Churchill: I took part in the Deaf Band experience for just a couple of weeks. I had responded to an advertisement from guitarist, Alex Chu, to play with The Deaf Band. It seemed like an opportunity to learn something new. So I packed up my bass guitar and amplifier and drove out to New Jersey to meet the band. We had prepared a couple of songs in advance, and when we started jamming, it sounded pretty good. Alex is a terrific lead guitar player, and I enjoyed watching "Knockin' on Heaven's Door" ASL-interpreted by Penelope Miller. It was a fantastic experience!

The music was fun, but incredibly *loud*! My bass was plugged into a serious, decibel packing Marshall half tower amp. So I used an earplug to protect my "good" ear during our rehearsals and performances. This completely muffled my high frequency hearing, so I was forced to constantly use my eyes to be sure I was in synch with the other musicians.

I was conscious throughout of my bass notes and the drums vibrating through my entire body. But overall, I'd say it probably wasn't so much different from your average rock concert experience. I think the Deaf audience enjoyed it very much, and I would love to do it again someday!

LEWIS MERKIN
Actor

It had been quite a few years since Lewis Merkin and I saw each other, so I thought it would be fun to chitchat with one of my favorite actors.

Raymond Luczak: Tell us a bit about your background.

Lewis Merkin: I grew up as the third generation in a Deaf family in Philadelphia. My maternal grandparents were immigrants from Kiev, Ukraine who had four children, two of whom were deaf: my uncle and my mother. My father was the only deaf one in his immediate family. Mom was educated at the Pennsylvania School for the Deaf; Dad, the oral public school. I have one brother who, like me, is technically hard of hearing. He went to the oral public school, while I was sent to the local public school. This was pre-mainstreaming: no interpreters, no notetakers, no other Deaf kids. My parents felt if you had enough hearing, it was best to assimilate into the hearing world as the Deaf world was too limiting. That's why my parents didn't encourage us to sign growing up, which is ironic considering that all their friends were Deaf, and we were exposed to ASL from day one. My early awkward signing belied my amazing receptive skills, but once I really started to associate with Deaf peers, it was as if a switch was turned on and the expressive ASL came very naturally and quickly.

Luczak: What led you to acting?

Merkin: I had childhood fantasies: placing myself on the screen opposite the stars of the day; the inevitable Oscar acceptance speech, etc. I took a summer theater course at a local playhouse during high school, which led to pursuing it in college. Because opportunities for Deaf actors were limited at California State University-Northridge, several of us were involved in creating productions so we could pursue our craft. One of these was Peter Shaffer's *Equus*, which got terrific reviews and garnered several awards including a Drama-Logue award for my work as Alan Strang. It was at this time that *Children of a Lesser God* was being cast. I had already auditioned for the part of Orin, but wasn't called back for a second audition until the director, Gordon Davidson, came to see *Equus*. Apparently, I was initially turned down because I spoke too well to play Orin, but after seeing my range I was asked if I could "deafen" my voice. That's easy! Ask any CODA! The rest was history: After a two-month run at a major theater in Los Angeles (L.A.), we transferred to Broadway where the show ran for over two years.

Luczak: What were some of the things you'd learned after that play became a success?

Merkin: So many things: It takes real discipline to do eight shows a week. You must be in excellent physical shape; you must be "on your toes" every moment you are on stage. I was lucky with both leads: Phyllis Frelich and John Rubenstein had won lead actor Tonys for their work. I worked on a daily basis with the best, watching how one can alter line readings to add more depth, find new meanings, and have fun while doing so. I was able to keep those lessons learned for all my subsequent acting work.

Luczak: Why did you move from Los Angeles to Seattle?

Merkin: After *Children*, I spent a number of years based in L.A., but on the road acting: the National Theatre of the Deaf, various regional theaters, and a stint with a British Deaf theatre company. When acting work was slow, I segued into becoming a community educator. I spent a few years as an HIV/AIDS educator in L.A. and then nearly five years as a sexual assault/domestic violence/oppression educator in Seattle.

Luczak: What brought you back to New York?

Merkin: While living in Seattle, I had an opportunity to co-write a play with Drew Emery, *Language of One*, as commissioned by a gay and lesbian theater company; Howie Seago directed it. A few years later New York Deaf Theater produced the show to great acclaim. As the lead in that production, I went to New York and I realized that I wasn't quite ready to give up my theatrical ambitions just yet. I then took the gamble of moving back to New York to reignite my acting career.

Luczak: Do you still audition, or have priorities changed for you?

Merkin: A funny thing happened on the way to . . . yes, in my first few years back in New York, I was focused on getting acting work and was involved in a few Off-Broadway and Off-Off Broadway productions. At the same time, I started to work as an interpreter to help pay the bills. It was then I realized how much interpreting had in common with acting: a love of language; parsing the true meaning of what was being said and being able to convey that with integrity and depth of meaning; the utilization of various parts of the brain simultaneously to ensure it all comes together seamlessly; and constant exposure to new experiences, people and places. Perfect for someone who has borderline ADD! I still audition, but I haven't pursued my acting at the level that I've focused on my interpreting work. I'm still a proud card-carrying member of Equity and SAG.

Luczak: Do you think that Deaf theater has changed, or has the hearing theater community changed over the years?

Merkin: There seems to be less opportunity these days: very few Deaf theater companies; more individuals focused on their own career rather than creating group projects; the economics are bad. Perversely, hearing theater companies are hiring hearing actors to play Deaf roles again. It's an uphill battle that one group of people is currently addressing in New York with mixed results. The New York Theatre Workshop's production of *The Heart is a Lonely Hunter* is opening in December with a hearing actor in the lead Deaf role. The producers met with the New York Deaf theater community and refused to reconsider the casting choice or entertain creative suggestions for keeping the casting while adding a Deaf actor into the piece. On the other hand, the producers of the upcoming Broadway revival of *The Miracle Worker* are opening up auditions for Deaf and blind actors to understudy Abigail Breslin, who will portray Helen Keller. Several articles on these issues have been published in various print and online media, and responses from the community at large have been unduly harsh: "It's just acting!" "Stop playing the PC police." Thirty years after Phyllis Frelich won her Tony and 25 years after Marlee Matlin won her Oscar, we should not be spending energy on this, but in encouraging opportunities for Deaf artists all around. I'd love to see more encouragement of Deaf writers from within the Deaf theater companies to help expand these opportunities for all. We also need our hearing allies in the industry to stand with us. With the explosion of Internet-based media, new opportunities abound. It's up to all of us, collectively, to expand our horizons and show the beauty of our Deaf culture to all.

ROSIE MAZIQUE
Patternmaker

I had the wonderful fortune of meeting Rosie when she came to Red Wing, Minnesota, to visit with her sister. I was struck by her vision of what she wanted to do with her life.

Raymond Luczak: When you and I met, you explained that you were "half-Deaf." Can you explain how you came up with that phrase?

Rosie Mazique: For a very long time I struggled with my self-identity when it came to my hearing. My family is so strongly rooted in Deaf culture that we, of course, take pride in what it means to be Deaf. However, I went to all mainstream schools, I had all hearing friends, spoken English is my primary language, and I have never needed to use hearing aids. I get by with my hearing loss in a way that made me feel I was hearing—at least in comparison to my family members. So for years, I went back and forth—I'm hearing, they would call me a "think-hearing" a terrible insult to me, so I would call myself "hearing impaired." Only recently did I learn that the term "hearing impaired" was still not the right term for me. Both of my parents are Deaf, both of my older siblings are Deaf, my maternal grandparents Deaf, and because of these people I am fluent in ASL and have had the privilege of experiencing life through a different lens and with a unique background. Simply calling myself "hearing impaired" only describes my inability to hear certain sounds, so where did my background fit into that term? Nowhere. I've decided to call myself "half-Deaf." "Half-Deaf" describes my lack of complete hearing ability, but it also infers that I have a Deaf Culture background.

Luczak: You've mentioned that you were studying for a degree in fashion.

Mazique: I'm currently pursuing a bachelor's degree in Fashion Design at Columbia College Chicago. I have one more semester to go until I graduate, and I have learned a lot. There are three tiers of business in the fashion industry. Tier one involves design—researching trends, designing new ones, and imagining entire collections for each season. Tier two involves construction, taking those designs, and mapping out the pieces to create a pattern that is sent to warehouses to be sewn and manufactured. This mapping is called patternmaking, which is the part of the industry I am interested in. Tier three is sales, sending those items to the stores, visual merchandising, etc.

Tier two interests me the most because it is the most hands-on. In my patternmaking classes, I take a sketch of a garment, be it a dress, jacket, blouse, skirt, or winter coat, and analyze how many pieces are required to assemble this garment. Does it have sleeves? How long are they? Where on the body does the hemline and waistline hit? Is there a lining? Pockets? All of these aspects and more must be considered before even beginning to create a pattern. The most difficult part of patternmaking is figuring out how to take fabric that begins in a two-dimensional flat state and ends up forming to the three-dimensional human body. It involves a lot of conceptualizing, measuring, and trial and error. The patternmaker is responsible for turning someone else's dream into a reality and creating a map that informs others how to recreate that exact same garment. They are also responsible for making sure the garments fit correctly on a range of body types. Side seams must hit at the side for every single person, pockets must be placed in exactly the right spot, and there absolutely cannot be any puckering or pulling. The patternmaker does so much that it is hard to fathom that not many people even know the patternmaker exists. Which reminds me of my favorite *Futurama* quote, "If you do something right, people won't be sure you've done anything at all."

Luczak: I was very struck by your simple vision: Why not have clothes for the disabled not only functional but also stylish? What led you to come up with that concept?

Mazique: My younger brother, Jacob, was born with many complications including spina bifida and cerebral palsy. He spent his life in a wheelchair and relied on others to dress him. I witnessed my mom's struggles with clothing my brother. We had to buy specific clothes with necklines to avoid blocking his trachea. He required oxygen tubes at birth and had a tracheastomy his whole life, which is why we had to buy clothing with the right necklines. Eventually he could breathe on his own and no longer required the oxygen at all times, but he continued to wear thermovents. We also had to ensure that the clothes he wore was made of materials that he was not allergic to and that were not harsh on his sensitive skin. He was allergic to latex, and believe it or not, a lot of children's clothing contains latex in the graphic images sewn or screen-printed on. Second, we had to make sure the clothes would not interfere with any of his medicinal aids such as his feeding tube and their movement. Every single t-shirt had to be a v-neck or a button-up so we could control where it would hit him on his neckline so as not to interfere with his breathing. Tops also needed to be loose enough so that it would not harm his g-button on his stomach that connected to his feeding tube. The biggest struggle with clothing was accessibility. It was hard to put clothes on Jacob. His arms and legs were stiff and inflexible which, unfortunately, would result in broken bones on occasion. Can you imagine breaking multiple bones over something as simple as putting your clothes on? It was heartbreaking.

Luczak: Can you go into detail about some of the things you'd need to think about when putting clothes together for disabled people?

Mazique: Seeing my brother's struggles made me realize that so many others are struggling just like him. Everyone deserves to pick out an outfit for the day, put it on with ease, wear it with ease, and feel good about themselves. I started my degree at Columbia College Chicago hoping to gain the technical skills I would need to learn how to adjust modern clothing to make it easier to put on, take off, and wear. Something as simple as larger zipper pulls could be viewed as a design choice, but it would actually help those with less motor skills dress themselves. Think of it this way—the round doorknob that requires a firm grip to hold and turn is not accessible, but a flat-handled doorknob is accessible because you can use your wrist, your elbow, or a stick to push it down and open that door. I would just like to introduce the same concept of accessibility to clothing, but accessibility is just the beginning. Eventually, fabrics can be modified to provide medicinal benefits, secret pockets, and hidden "canals" in clothing could help maintain oxygen tubing, hold emergency medicine, and much more.

People in wheelchairs are literally sitting all day, and it is incredibly uncomfortable sitting on a lot of pocket seams, so pants with no back pockets are very important as well as a higher back waistline to provide adequate coverage. However, these beneficiary details might make the pants less stylish, which highlights the importance of a designer introducing new details to create style despite the differences between clothes simply meant for style and clothes made for those with physical disabilities. One should never be forced to resort to sweatpants and tees just because it is too hard for them to put on or wear items that are more stylish. I believe everyone deserves to right to make themselves feel good if they want, and I would like to expand the fashion industry to include this new demographic of people with physical disabilities.

Luczak: What are some of the things you've learned along the way while trying to execute that vision?

Mazique: I have learned that there is a lot of room to grow when it comes to designing clothes for people with disabilities. Some companies with business models based on the idea of accessible clothing exist, but most are based online and run out of home or their target markets are senior citizens. The industry is aware that there is a need for this type of market. Research has been done on developing new fabrics to help with circulation for those with diabetes, and companies are coming out with bras made for women who are currently undergoing treatment for breast cancer or who are healing.

The main issue with clothing for those with physical disabilities is that our economy is based on mass marketing, and this particular faction of the fashion industry would be heavily based on custom work; however, this does not mean that there isn't hope.

ROBBIE WILDE
DJ and Producer

An article about him popped up on my Facebook's newsfeed. After reading it, I reached out to him with some questions.

Raymond Luczak: Can you tell us a bit about how you became late-deafened?

Robbie Wilde: At the age of seven, I had severe ear infections in both ears. After months of high fevers, ear infections, and medication, my parents weren't able to afford the medicine anymore. The ear infections and high fever had caused damage to my ears, leaving me with no hearing in my right ear, and damage in my left. It wasn't until the age of 11 when my mother took me to an audiologist that my hearing loss was confirmed. In turn, the first four years of public school were filled with misunderstandings about this. My teachers believed my poor learning capabilities were the result of ADD [Attention Deficit Disorder], but in reality, communication—or lack thereof—was the reason. This misdiagnosis would then be relayed to my parents, furthering the wave of misunderstandings. Quite a frustrating cycle.

Luczak: Have you ever interacted with other Deaf people who signed? What was that like for you? Did you feel like you could identify with them?

Wilde: I have many friends in the deaf/hard of hearing (HOH) community; some being very close friends of mine. I don't typically sign, yet I can understand bits and pieces in conversation. We definitely relate with one another regarding our communication struggles with the hearing community, and the judging associated with our hearing situations. But we help each other through motivation and outside-the-box ideas on how to build the bridge between the hearing and deaf communities.

Luczak: Do you know ASL?

Wilde: I do sign, but not fluently. When we received confirmation about my hearing loss, I had already been in the hearing public schools from kindergarten to third grade. I was capable of passing the classes during that time, which led to the decision of continuing my education in the public schools. Nothing is more important to my mother than the best education an individual may receive. The journey of being a deaf/HOH student in a hearing public school could have never been successful if it wasn't for her. In her mind, anything was possible with time and dedication. And that's exactly what we did all the way through college.

Luczak: What kinds of music did you enjoy while growing up? Why those particular kinds?

Wilde: I love all genres of music, which is why I choose to be an "open format" DJ. I grew up in England, Portugal, Venezuela, and America. Such exposure to different genres and cultures of music have helped me understand and appreciate music with an open mind. Throughout my childhood, as one could imagine, doctors would stress the dangers of headphones or music at high volumes in order to protect the remaining hearing I had on my left. The rest of the world is quiet for me, so loud music was something I needed at all times. I would steal my father's headphones and cassesette player and walk to school trying to listen with the volume at max. But music was always around me and impossible to be away from. My father is a music junkie, I played in the school bands, my middle brother is an insane drummer/guitarist/songwriter, my youngest brother is a violinist, and we're Portuguese. There's always someone at home playing the harmonica/guitar and singing to the day's work.

Luczak: Tell us about your first DJ job. What was that like?

Wilde: My first "official" gig was at a placed called Destino Lounge (now known as Vida Lounge) in Elizabeth, NJ. The energy and response from the crowd was great. A small venue with huge energy. Very personal with the crowd. After that night I asked the owner if I could play as much as possible. I wanted to learn the craft as much as I could. And the DJs there were the best anyone can learn from. A very traditional house music cultured group. I was a resident there for about four years. In the beginning I was deejaying while the bar backs would prepare for the night. But I did everything possible to learn and be around the booth. I studied beat-matching, song selection, house music culture, and crowd control from Big Mike, EvR, G-Wiz, BlaQwell, and Haelmik. And finally Alexander Technique explained to me the importance of the cross-fader and production. I was very lucky to be around such knowledgeable DJs with the proper experience of the art and culture. Being around them all the time helped me to learn and grow into the DJ and producer I am today.

Luczak: How did you progress from that gig to what you do now?

Wilde: From my first gig? A lot. It's been a nice, hardworking, dedicated ten years or so of only focusing on the art. I took this full time within the first year of my journey. I'm always learning, always paying my dues. But there is always room to grow, and someone to prove it to. I spent two hours a day, twice a week, for two years with DJ Shiftee (2x World Supremacy DMC Champion) at Dubspot NYC, learning the art, details, and culture of scratching. 10,000 hours and counting! To learn and grow in all I do is something I seek on a daily basis. It's a way of life.

Luczak: How do you know which songs to play? Do you listen to all kinds of music in your "down" time and make notes of which ones might be good choices for DJ gigs? What do you look for in "good" songs? Or is it just all about the beats?

Wilde: When it comes to song selection, I use my customized ear monitor that Starkey Hearing Foundation hooked me up with to review and research my music. I still can't make out the lyrics on songs too well, but I do my research online. I search, purchase, and download tracks that I feel would complement my sets. I have a whole system that I go through in order to prepare, but rest assured, I put my time in. What takes a hearing DJ one hour to do will take me at least six, but I'll finish those six hours without stopping until EVERYTHING IS PERFECT. I am about the "beats," but I understand that I cater to both communities when it comes to my sets. I'm prepared in all aspects of the music and communities.

They say, "When you're sad, you understand the lyrics; when you're happy, you enjoy the beats." I'm always happy. LOL

Luczak: In another interview, you've said this: "Music is not all about hearing." Can you explain what this means for you?

Wilde: To get the full experience of a record, it's not only about the lyrics; it's also about getting the full feeling of the music itself. Producers spend a lot time on the sounds they choose to create the music. Each instrument is calculated to their emotions they want portrayed in their tracks. So take a "listen" to the overall song, "feel" the journey the producer is taking you on, every instrument and sound used is important in gaining the full experience of the song! So crank it up! Feel the beat! Make any floor your dance floor!

Luczak: Have you ever thought about getting cochlear implants, or do you think that would mess up with your creativity as a DJ since it's all "muscle memory" now?

Wilde: As a child we considered it, but couldn't. I don't know if it would have altered my creativity. I'm deaf/HOH and figured out a way not to mess up with my condition now. I wouldn't necessarily assume that creativity would get affected by cochlear implants. With dedication, time, passion, and most important, education on the subject, I believe anything is possible. Plus, you never know what kinda crazy sounds can come out from an individual's mind. Your mind is a very powerful tool.

DAWN STOYANOFF
Theater Director

Even though I've never met Dawn Stoyanoff in person, I liked her web site enough to know that this was someone I wanted to know better. What did her mission statement say? "DawnStage Productions is a collaborative theater company that works to transform disability and diversity stereotypes by promoting artistic, excellence, social justice, and diversity."

Raymond Luczak: How did you become deaf? How did your family deal with it?

Dawn Stoyanoff: I was born Deaf. My mom dealt with it pretty well unlike most parents at the time. Like most families, we grieved, denied, and eventually learned to accept it as a part of life. As a mother, she would do anything to make sure that I was happy. She would send me to socialize with the Deaf Community since I was two years old. At the time, most people would make sure sign language was not allowed in their households, my mom allowed sign language. She welcomed my Deaf friends, and often my Deaf friends would be jealous about the kind of mother she was.

Luczak: How did you get involved with theater?

Stoyanoff: I always wanted to be an actor however, my parents were pretty realistic and suggested that I needed a good and solid background to fall on in case I couldn't make it in theater. So I went to college, got my B.A. degree in Psychology with an emphasis in Women Studies, went to direct children's shows while working full time at the South Dakota School for the Deaf, but with theater on my mind. When I started working at Itasca Community College, I got my first paid job as an actor and consultant for a production of *Children of a Lesser God*. The minute I was on stage, I fell in love and the director saw how good I was on stage. At the time, however, I knew I didn't want to be poor and living on the street so I stuck with jobs that were reliable. My family's poor and I had to support myself.

When I worked in South Dakota, I seized opportunities to direct children's plays for five years. When I met my husband and fell in love, I quit my job and moved to Seattle. I always wanted a master's degree in Theater. I applied to a major university and didn't get in because the competition was tough—500 candidates had competed for 15 places. Finally, I applied at Western Washington University for a M.A. in Theater Arts and got in. All together, I have been involved since 1992, off and on, either directing or acting. Once I set my foot onstage in theater, I belong there. I love the art of storytelling.

Luczak: What shows have you done? And what were some of your favorite parts?

Stoyanoff: I directed and acted in many shows since 1992. I enjoyed directing *Jeopardy Gaping* and *Love Person* because women wrote these. *Love Person* was most challenging for me as a co-director because we had to create "closed captioning" onstage with three projectors and dealing with one green actor (she did an awesome job!). *Jeopardy Gaping* had a lot of bloody messes to clean up (part of the script!) and it dealt with issues that I enjoy (more like thinking outside the box).

My favorite role was Eleanor in *Big Love*. I had an interpreter on stage with me. The cast was awesome. It was a non-signing hearing cast. When I auditioned for the part, I muttered to myself that I love this character. I didn't expect the director to overhear me, but the interpreter voiced my remarks. Eleanor is big on love. She loves life and being loved. The director cast me because I'm human first before being a Deaf woman. I love playing a character and portraying her humanity. The script didn't call for a Deaf character, and that gave extra meaning to why I loved this character. It went beyond that identity.

Luczak: Why did you become a stage director?

Stoyanoff: I was drawn into directing when I was working at the school for the Deaf and then later in Seattle's Deaf Youth Drama Program. I always followed my heart. One thing lead to another that made me realized that theater fits me. I often tell people, "Why work in jobs you hate? Better love your job and you'll stay with it for a long time." If I didn't love it, I would have quit a long time ago. After I paint the canvas on stage, I'm a nervous wreck, sitting on the edge of my seat rooting for the actors to do a great job. That's why I tend to sit behind the audience, hiding. I just love the excitement and chaos of putting on a show.

JILL BEEBOUT
Theater Manager

Deaf theater continues to be a vital part of our community because, other than ASL storytelling, it remains the most direct form of artistic expression in ASL. After having worked as a playwright for Illuminations … Theatre with the Deaf, I was very impressed by the fact that the theater company had survived 20 years, an enviable record for any small non-profit theater company. In spite of having worked with its general manager, Jill Beebout, we never had time to sit down and talk about her work at Illuminations; she was always too busy! But we finally made time.

Raymond Luczak: Did you have theater training?

Beebout: I have a B.A. in Theater from the University of Northern Iowa (UNI). My focus was Tech/Design. The best thing about my major was that I was exposed to such a wide variety of skill areas. I've worked as a welder, painter, props master, stage manager, and production manager. I didn't really have the innate skill or drive to be onstage. While I love the theater world, I needed something more secure than the odd acting role, and I realized that there are so many more jobs "backstage."

Luczak: So what led you to ASL and the Deaf community?

Beebout: I've always had an interest in languages and I tend to be a fairly visual person, so ASL just held a total fascination for me. Unlike most hearing people who work in the Deaf community, I didn't have any real exposure to ASL or the community until I was an adult.

I became disenchanted with the regional theater world and needed to do something new, so I enrolled in an Interpreter Training Program (ITP) at Houston Community College. I knew very little sign at that time, and figured that would be the best way to learn. After UNI, I was offered an internship at the Dallas Theatre Center and then hired full-time in Production Management. I met my husband there, and we eventually came to Houston when he was hired by the Alley Theater.

Luczak: How did you get involved with Illuminations?

Beebout: During my first semester in the ITP, Illuminations started offering classes in ASL Acting, Theatre Crafts and Media Production. I decided since theater was already an area I was comfortable with, the classes would be a good opportunity for me to get more ASL exposure, so I took the acting class. Then during the second semester that the classes were offered, I team-taught the Theatre Crafts class and I've been working with Illuminations ever since.

At that time it was still Illuminations ... Theatre with the Deaf. Susan Jackson, the current Artistic Director of Illuminations, had just been hired as the Project Director of OPTICA (Our Paths Together: Initiating Cultural Access). This was a program established through a three-year grant from the U.S. Department of Education before that point Illuminations had never had full-time staff. OPTICA was an educational program that encouraged Deaf, Hard of Hearing and hearing people to interact and develop skills in theater and media as well as their knowledge of ASL and Deaf culture. It also included monthly movie nights (featuring movies/videos that highlighted Deaf performers/characters).

Since its inception, Illuminations has offered sign language interpretation for Houston area theaters. Illuminations also works with area children's theaters to offer shadow interpreting of productions, so that the signing performers are onstage right along with the speaking actors. This is very popular with the Deaf kids, getting to see someone onstage signing just like they do.

In recent years, Illuminations has also independently produced four plays involving a combination of Deaf and hearing performers. Three of these plays were written by Deaf playwrights such as Michele M. Verhoosky.

Luczak: So when OPTICA ended, you just went with Susan into Illuminations?

Beebout: Before OPTICA, Illuminations focused on theatrical interpreting and/or shadowing productions with other Houston area theaters. Actually, after working with OPTICA for the first year, Illuminations received a grant from Houston Endowment Inc. that enabled them to hire a director for the new ASL Storytelling program, and they offered me that job.

Luczak: Were you able to make any breakthroughs in increasing audiences as well as their appreciation of that genre?

Beebout: The two areas of the storytelling program that I am most proud of is the development of Bi-Modal storytelling and the Hand Held Tales (HHT) at School program. Bi-Modal storytelling utilizes a team of one Deaf and one hearing storyteller, working together to reach hearing and Deaf audiences. This continues to be the basis for the Hand Held Tales program. The HHT at School program uses storytelling as an educational tool.

Luczak: What advice would you give if someone from the signing community wanted to set up a theater company of their own in their own city?

Beebout: This may sound odd, but make sure you have an audience. Just because there are deaf people (or any people) in your area, doesn't mean they will go see a play. Audience outreach (and education) is crucial. Then once you have established that there is an audience out there, start with something small and do it really well. But you don't have to reinvent the wheel—try setting up a co-production with an existing theater. It's a great way to get your feet wet without having to do everything yourself.

STACIA RICE
Theater Producer

I had the good fortune of seeing a wonderful Torch Theater production of William Gibson's *The Miracle Worker* in which Shelby Flannery gave an intelligent performance as Helen Keller. I was more taken with Stacia Rice's approach to playing Helen's teacher, Annie Sullivan. Her character seemed like a troublemaker, and what's more, Stacia was on a crusade not only for Helen but also for accessible theater through her new Torch Theater in her real life.

Raymond Luczak: You say that Torch has a newly refined mission: "Super Accessible Theater." What did you mean by that?

Stacia Rice: What I mean by super accessible theater is that I hope to be artistic in our approach to accessibility. It is my dream to continue what we have started with *The Miracle Worker*. I hope to have ASL interpretation offered at every show. I want our interpreters to be on the stage, as they are now, and a part of our cast. I want them to be in our curtain call because they are as much of the show as any of our actors. I want our blind patrons to be able to choose between many Audio Description Nights. I want to continue to offer Tactile Tours for people with visual impairments (this is a pre-show tour where our blind patrons can come onto the set and touch props and costumes). I want our lobby displays to include Braille descriptions for photographs and representative swatches of fabric. I want to have valet parking available for people with special physical considerations. And I want to be able to remove our entire front row to make space for wheelchairs.

I would love to say "completely accessible theater" someday. But being able to say that will take some funding. I'm on that—I'm devoted to making that happen. But right now we'll settle for super accessible and know that we're still forward in our thinking.

Luczak: Why did you choose *The Miracle Worker*? Do you think the story has a lot of relevance for the DeafBlind community today?

Rice: Actually, I didn't choose the play because of its relevance to any one community. I chose it for its relevance to humans as a whole. There's something in it for everyone, I think. It's about perserverence, about rising above life's challenges and, ultimately, about giving. Everyone in the play has a need and everyone in the play has a gift. At some point during the play we get to see both of those things tackled with each character. I like to think that the play carries specific relevence to the DeafBlind community and maybe to the blind and Deaf communities as well. But the real reason I chose it is because it speaks to the fact that we are all the same. Everyone has their own set of challenges (emotional, physical, or both), but we all need to be respected and we all need to connect. This play lets those things happen.

Luczak: Did you learn new things about being partially blind while researching the part of Annie Sullivan?

Rice: I actually played a blind woman in *Wait Until Dark* earlier this year and did a little research on Annie's condition for this show. I learned that you need to be an incredibly strong human to deal with the loss of any of your senses. Annie has a special kind of perseverance, I think, having dealt with the loss of her sight and growing up in the State Almshouse, where she was really left to defend herself from all sorts of people and situations.

The only performance of Annie that I've ever seen is the film version with Anne Bancroft. She was a very powerful actress, and I think she did a remarkable job. My version of Annie is slightly rougher than hers. Maybe a little scrappier. And the only reason my Annie is this way is based on some of the things I read. She had a mouth on her that got her into a lot of trouble. I tried to capture that in this production.

Luczak: Any words of advice on meeting the daunting challenges of making a show truly accessible?

Rice: I think it's worth it for any of us creating theater (or any kind of art) to try and open it to as many people as possible. There's such a neutral world that exists in theater—on and off the stage. Why not make a statement there by making it inclusive to as many people as possible? It's hard work, yes. But I have to say that one of my proudest moments in theater so far was when I saw the light cue for our interpreters and heard the audience applaud them as they made their entrance for Act 2 on opening night. I knew that they were a part of the cast when that happened. And if they're a part of the cast, and our Audio Describer is part of the cast, then everyone in the theater is a member of one audience. One. Not the Deaf audience and the hearing audience. *One* audience. And if we're all one cast and one audience and we're all sharing one experience, then we're back to my tree-hugging hippie attitude about the healing energy of theater. See? It works.

ETHAN SINNOTT
Scenic Designer

Every time I see photographs of his work onstage, I'm always in awe, and apparently I'm not the only one! He's very much in demand around the Washington, D.C. area, so I was quite fortunate that he had time for my questions.

Raymond Luczak: What was your background like?

Ethan Sinnott: I was born Deaf into a hearing family. My parents learned sign language not long after finding out, and I'm a mainstreaming product. I didn't become a true citizen of the Deaf world until college.

Luczak: Which came first for you: drawing/visualizing and/or seeing theater productions?

Sinnott: Drawing/visualizing. Those genes run strong through my mother, her brother, and late maternal grandfather, a first-generation Dutch-American descended from craftsmen, farmers, and furniture-makers in an area near the border with Belgium. It's a natural ability I inherited, which I think has been heightened to compensate for my being Deaf.

My mother's side of the family has always been artistic. My grandfather used to create crazy-accurate model ships from scratch, such as Spanish galleons, 19th-century English warships, and even the wharf of Rockport, MA, despite never having gone to art school. My uncle taught painting at the Boston Museum of Fine Arts School for over three decades, and he still has his studio near Fenway Park. My mother has been creating quilts in the American folk art style as far back as I can remember.

Luczak: Were you always interested in theater? Were you able to follow the dialogue, or did that not matter so much?

Sinnott: I have always been instinctually drawn to the role and use of images in the telling of stories, and theater is one of those mediums where the power of the image—one, or multiple, or in layers—helps amplify a story metaphorically, sequentially, symbolically, and thematically. You see a lot of that in Renaissance frescoes.

I do remember very well the first time, as a child, my parents took me to the National Technical Institute for the Deaf (NTID) to see a play with signing Deaf actors. It was *A Christmas Carol* with Patrick Graybill, one of the original members of the National Theatre of the Deaf, in the role of Scrooge. I thought it nothing short of miraculous—I'd grown up during a pre-ADA time when almost nothing was closed-captioned. I was deep into comic books, watched formulaic TV series based on comic books and cartoons (such as Lou Ferrigno in *The Incredible Hulk* and *Spider-Man and His Amazing Friends*) where I could follow the basic plot absent accessible dialogue, and my father would take me to the movies and interpret for me the best he could—*E. T.*, Harryhausen's *Clash of the Titans, Superman II, The Empire Strikes Back*, and so on.

Being the only Deaf student at my hearing middle/high school, their annual play would usually be a musical—the audition notices would often read COME PREPARED TO SING A SONG (with piano accompaniment). That was intimidating. That is such a sentence wedded to the hearing world that takes for granted the spoken word, and I did not want to humiliate myself singing unintelligibly in recognizably Deaf speech in front of people who had no intention of casting me. At some point I found out about a competition open to high school students sponsored by, ironically, the local chapter of the English-Speaking Union. Basically, we had to perform a soliloquy and sonnet—I saw it as a chance to be an actor on my terms.

I chose for my soliloquy the one by Richard of Gloucester at the end of *3 Henry VI*, right after he's killed Henry VI, with an unexpected outcome: I finished as national runner-up at the Lincoln Center in New York City. That was the spark of validation I needed to pursue my passion for theater.

I acted through my college years, on the same stage where I had seen *A Christmas Carol* a decade earlier as well as in a local community Shakespeare outfit, but ultimately, due to my growing sense that there were more than enough Deaf actors, or Deaf people wanting to be actors, but not enough Deaf people in positions of artistic and creative power in theatre and film, my interests transcended being an actor.

I didn't set out to be a scene designer, but to be a director, an artist working in theater, and in some kind of "producer" role, I just fell into scene design as a means to that end. In many ways, being a scene designer has helped me add a new dimension as a theater artist. I love the collaborative aspect of the design process, though—I consider myself lucky enough to have worked with a lot of gifted people, most of all the lighting designers. My experiences as an actor have helped me with my scene designs, too—I try to get inside their heads when it's time to turn the design concept into something more concrete. It's simple psychology—the quality of the scene design more or less does have an effect on an actor's performance.

When I take in a non-interpreted hearing production—and I go to a lot of those—I usually read the script before I go, and I pay more attention to its stage image and visual flow than its onstage dialogue. I leave with strong feelings of whether a production was effective or not—did it have a clear sense of vision, did the pieces come together, did it "flow," did it amplify the story? Often I find myself initially baffled by universally enthusiastic reviews given to a production I thought was clichéd or pedestrian or stilted in its staging, or worse. Then I remind myself what are audiences responding to? Primarily to what they hear. What the hell do I know about that? I'm responding to primarily what I see. And there you have it: the same production is experienced as two separate realities.

Luczak: You went to the Rochester Institute of Technology, correct?

Sinnott: I went to RIT over my father's objections. As I'd grown up in Rochester, he rightfully felt that I needed to experience life in a new city. I had Boston University, Carnegie Mellon, Columbia, and Yale on my list, but I no longer had the desire to be the only Deaf student at my school anymore, and not at the expense of my education.

Luczak: What are some of the more common misconceptions about theater scenic design? Do you think your deafness is an advantage to your career? If not, how has it hindered your career? Or have things improved for you?

Sinnott: It's somehow perceived as an unserious job whereas other people are actually working real jobs, as if the arts are no less an occupation.

Theater is collaborative, and it's not like I tell everyone in our first meeting— the director, the other designers, the rest of the production team—"This is the set," which perpetuates the silly mythology of the exalted artist. Everyone has opinions and thoughts about the production, its direction, its aesthetic, its meaning, and certainly, designs are not immune. A successful, marketable designer—in any theater discipline—needs to be a skilled collaborator and negotiator who is able to navigate all those egos and opinions toward consensus, and there's no overstating the value of tact. Some production teams are handpicked by the play's director; others are assembled by the production manager. Some teams are familiar with each other, having worked together in the past; some teams may have never worked with each other, and, in this case, chemistry is a crapshoot. Piss off a director—or a production manager—and don't act surprised if your gigs dwindle. My final set designs are, on average, third or fourth drafts based on everyone's feedback.

Complicating matters more is the fact I'm Deaf, the only one in a room or theater full of hearing people, most with little to no experience interacting with Deaf people—and working with an ASL interpreter for the first time. During these kinds of meetings, the pace is brisk, freewheeling, with a lot of overlapping talk. It's challenging enough to keep up even with experienced interpreters I have a preexisting rapport with.

I'd like to quote from my web site: "As a designer, the fact I'm Deaf has always influenced and informed my approach to unit sets as stage environments with the ability to seemingly transform themselves through scenic elements manipulated by actors, lighting, and/or machinery, with the goal of creating opportunities for visual rhythm and flow, a musicality in itself, rather than visual inertia and static associated with most unit sets. I think that's in no small part due to the fact we are living in an era where the power of visually-oriented media—in all its forms—has been ascendant for some time now, and it aligns perfectly with the daily streams of consciousness familiar to Deaf people such as myself." So when I design, I'm designing not only for the directors I work with, but for the lighting designers I work with, and for random Deaf theater audience members, too.

Luczak: A few years back you made a big push for a stronger recognition and need for Deaf theater. Do you feel that situation has improved? Or has it gotten worse?

Sinnott: This is a loaded question, and I fear that my answer will not be enough at this time. It's a complicated question, and these are complicated circumstances. We need to do a series of conversations on all of this. So far, I think we're in a holding pattern, but we're clearly in a race against time, geography, technology, and to an extent, political fallout at both state and national levels.

The state of American Deaf theater, presently, continues to be endangered, exacerbated by scant opportunities existing in the mainstream for early-career Deaf theater artists. There is an urgent need for mentoring and support of early-career Deaf theater artists in the field, as no such system exists, yet. The situation is hindered by the fact that as the professional theater and film fields consist of predominantly hearing people, there are too few hearing theater professionals willing to take a flyer on a young, talented, early-career Deaf theater artist; conversely, there is little semblance of a cohesive national community of Deaf theater artists in which an operational infrastructure is in place to ensure the continuous, uninterrupted development of successive generations of Deaf theater talent (transferable to film), not just as actors, but across the board.

We lost Phyllis Frelich earlier this year, many Deaf theater trailblazers have aged, the National Theatre of the Deaf is a shell of its heyday, and Deaf West continues to persevere the best it can. Where's that bridge between our past and present toward our future? There's an urgency here, and times like these need more than ever those of us who have ingrained artistic collaboration as a value, able to see the larger picture: we are representatives of an underrepresented people and culture in every walk of life, and we owe it to ourselves to mentor those who come after us, so they can mentor those who come after them, thus keeping Deaf theater traditions alive, yet evolving them through artistic experimentation. It's not practical to remain clusters and pockets of individuals any longer: we need to find a way to learn how to become an ecosystem with scope and vision, and collectively, own our fate.

As difficult and highly individualized as every Deaf theater artist's journey may have been to rise above it all and be recognized, once you get there, that's when the lure to get too comfortable intensifies—whether by a string of successes, continuous praise, what have you—and in that moment, it's important to remember that you are no longer doing this for yourself anymore. By getting where you are, whether you want it or not, you have become an ambassador, an inspiration, and a role model to others not unlike yourself seeking all of the above.

OF QUILL AND SOUL

KRISTEN RINGMAN
Author

I first became aware of Kristen Ringman when she sent in a breathtaking excerpt from her novel-in-progress *Makara* for my anthology *Eyes of Desire 2*. Some years later, I read her novel in its entirety and loved it so much that I *had* to publish it. *Makara* went on to become a Lambda Literary Award finalist for Debut Fiction.

Raymond Luczak: If I recall correctly, you were born hearing. You grew up with a deaf mother. What was that like?

Kristen Ringman: My mother went deaf soon after I was born. She didn't have a second child after me because she was afraid of something happening to me or another child and her not hearing us. This wasn't a very empowering introduction to my own hearing loss, which happened gradually from age six until I was 20 or so. I did learn to speak early and articulate my words in a way that made it easier for my mother to read my lips, because she never learned ASL while I was growing up. She loved to tell me stories. This was empowering. Her spoken storytelling, which may have been one way of maintaining her hearing identity, did empower me to love storytelling as well and search for my own stories. I began learning ASL at the age of 13 through summer Deaf camps, and became in love with traveling partly because my mother was scared of it. In some ways, her fears prompted me to never see deafness as a disability because it was so disabling for her, and I didn't want to live a life in fear.

In summer camp, signing was something everyone was either learning or using proficiently, and I remember loving the equality of it and the adventure of learning how to sing song lyrics with my hands. I embraced that small piece of the Deaf community as a teenager, but I didn't really understand the Deaf community's complexities until I was in Peace Corps Kenya's Deaf Education Program, where I was first immersed in ASL (and also Kenyan Sign Language) in my everyday life. That period was the only time I used ASL more than spoken English and considered not voicing anymore very seriously so that I could be more "Deaf" rather than just "deaf."

Now I am in the middle, and I often move back and forth. I've met more Deaf people who've closed themselves off from Hearing culture, and I know I can't do that myself, at least not entirely. Deaf culture is still a beautiful thing, but I've recently realized that it might not be as much "home" to me as I first thought it was as a teen and in my first months in Peace Corps. I have lived in so many other countries besides America that I've come to be more comfortable when I am in other countries or "not at home," because nowhere ever really feels 100% mine and understood. Even in Deaf culture, I feel a bit outside of it. I have stronger ideas now about the integration of Deaf and Hearing cultures rather than letting them remain apart, because I feel so connected to both cultures. I still voice and I often use ASL at the same time, which many Deaf people have told me is wrong or disrespectful, but at the same time, those people also say that I'm supposed to communicate however I am most comfortable, which is conflicting. I always feel that conflict inside of myself, like I am betraying my own culture every single day. My son is hearing and also signs, and it is often easier to talk to him with both languages simultaneously. I still stress over him not learning proper ASL. Some days I don't voice. Some days I voice more than I sign. I suppose this keeps me in between the Deaf and Hearing worlds, hovering, and not really joining either one.

Luczak: Tell me about the first time you started to realize that yes, indeed, you were meant to be a writer.

Ringman: I always wrote stories in my diary, but I was seven when I first wrote a "real story," about swimming in the ocean and a shark biting me in the neck and me going to Heaven. I went on to write poem after poem, from age ten until now, and longer and longer stories until I began writing novels. I probably realized I was meant to be a writer most profoundly when I was ten. My first poem was about two lovers on the beach deciding whether to open a door to love and then missing it. Writing felt magical. It opened not just the door to love, but to all the doors. I could go anywhere in my mind and weave the story of it onto the page like a sorcerer.

Luczak: What was attending Goddard College like?

Ringman: At first I thought it was a "hippie school," which fit my personality, but I was worried it wouldn't challenge me as a writer as much as Brown University, my first choice. After the first semester, however, I was blown away. Kenny Fries was my first advisor, and he was disabled so he felt kindred to me (though I didn't really consider my deafness a disability by that time). He fought hard to ensure my accessibility whenever it came into question, and he inspired me to be proud of my deafness and use it to make my writing better. I had ASL interpreters at Goddard for the first time in my life and found them to be amazing. Even at night, when I didn't have my interpreters by my side, I felt most "at home" among my fellow students of writing. Many of them learned sign language much faster than my non-writer friends, and I still long for that intense sense of community that surpassed Deaf culture for me by far. I dream of one day teaching at Goddard, and I'd recommend it to any Deaf writer as an incredible program that will change your life. I do feel that the slogan for Goddard that used to be on its T-shirts was spot on: "All the people from High School who were ostracized because they were weird." (So that would be another criteria for my recommendation—any weird deaf writer!)

Luczak: What prompted you to tell the story that is *Makara*? What have you learned from that process?

Ringman: I wrote *Makara* during my time at Goddard without planning it. It started as an entirely lyrical work, a novel in poetry and love song to India, Ireland, Venice, and women. So many of my experiences living in those countries as well as my closeness with my father have become encapsulated in some form or another within the pages of that book. I also needed such a long space to have a female love affair, because so many of my lesbian relationships have been short, so *Makara* was my way to release my own yearnings onto the page. It gradually became more prosaic over time, which scared me because I was afraid my poetic words couldn't survive in prose form. But *Makara* itself became stronger. I learned that I do need to write novels, perhaps more insistently than poems, because I want to sneak poetry into everything. I want fiction readers to become dizzy with the lyrical possibilities that fiction can be stretched to contain. And I want to write characters that make people fall in love or weep or scream, not just during one or two pages of verse, but for hundreds of pages. I want people to forget they are even reading anymore.

Luczak: Do you think that your Deafness is a major part of your writing, or is it just a part of who you are?

Ringman: My Deafness is a part of who I am and because of that, it is also a part of my writing. I agree with many other Deaf writers that there just aren't enough books out there with deaf protagonists and I want to change that with my writing. I won't always write from a deaf point-of-view, but I do wish to consistently include both deaf and LGBT characters within my writing because of their notorious underrepresentation in literature. The world needs more stories from people who are marginalized. I also wish to always write about other cultures because I personally don't want to live in a world dominated by Western culture, and my world isn't just around me; it's also the worlds I create on the page, too.

NICK STURLEY
Author

Some years ago I interviewed Nick Sturley about an app featuring British Sign Language (BSL) translations of classic stories. I decided to follow up from there.

Raymond Luczak: Is the story app, *Tales from Signtown*, still available?

Nick Sturley: To cut a very long story short, this project has been stalled, if not abandoned. Back in 2008, DeafEducate, a small independent publisher in the UK, approached me to write an ebook series for them. The idea was that the ebook—a book with a small CD containing the BSL translation of the text—would be distributed to deaf schools so that deaf children could learn English better by reading the text and watching the BSL translation.

I agreed to do it; however, I suggested that an iPhone app be created to include both the text and BSL translation. Rather than sitting in front of a PC at school and watching the translation, deaf children could use the iPhone and iPad. We would add more text/BSL stories in smartphones and tablet devices over time. The 24-volume series would consist of the classic fairy tale stories such as "Red Riding Hood," "Jack and the Beanstalk," "Cinderella," "Puss in Boots," "The Ugly Duckling," and so on, but with deaf characters centered in a town called Signtown. The characters would interact with each other in the town, like a Deaf community would, but also tell their own respective stories. For example, Red Riding Hood's best friend is Goldilocks who fancies Jack the Beanstalk. Red Riding Hood would encounter the Big Bad Wolf, who would happen to be the same one in Three Little Pigs and is wanted for assaulting the grandmother. Little Match Girl would appear in some of the stories, begging and selling matches for money prior to her own tragic story later in the series, and so on. The entire 24–volume series had its own story arc that would end with a long, thrilling climax based on a truly delightful, but emotional, fairy tale story that I won't reveal right now. Unfortunately, DeafEducate ran into financial troubles by the end of 2010. The series stopped on volume eight although I had written 12 by that point.

However, I have successfully obtained the rights to *Tales From Signtown* earlier this year. I'm hoping to reboot it into a 24-chapter book with brand new illustrations, and perhaps include a DVD of BSL translations. I still strongly believe this will be a unique reading and viewing experience for the children—deaf or hearing—and adults young at heart. I do not know when I'll restart it, but I will finish what I've started!

Luczak: About ten years ago you worked on a novel called *Milan*. I seem to recall that it was a very difficult book to write. Why was that?

Sturley: I wrote and self-published it in October 2003. It's a science fiction fantasy centered around an actual key event in Deaf history: the infamous Milan 1880 Congress. It was a very difficult book to write because it was my first one. The story has a very complex structure because it involves time travel, surprise plot twists involving a large number of characters, actual moments from Deaf history, and so on. It was important to me that the book be written in an accessible style so that the reader could follow the story. I also included a visual glossary, showing illustrations of key characters and architecture from the story, so that deaf readers can digest them from the text descriptions.

The book was very well received. However, I have just started to rework it with several changes in the action and dialogue, and correct some historical errors, particularly the Milan Congress itself, as the order of the proceedings was incorrect. I found a very rare book reporting the whole day-by-day proceedings a year and half after I published *Milan*. I also hope to have brand new illustrations and work with another publisher to bring it out, but I'm not sure if it will be self-published again. As many authors know, book publishing has changed quite considerably in recent years, and it has become even more difficult to make money from selling books. I'll still rework the book, and then we'll see. I'm doing it for the next generation.

Luczak: Your second book is called *Innocents of Oppression*. What inspired you to write it?

Sturley: Back in 2000, I had a dream about two deaf teenage boys sitting on the grass in front of my old boarding school, signing. One was older and had dark hair, and the other had blond hair. I didn't know who they were, but this dream had put in the first seed of what would become probably the biggest Deaf novel ever written by a Deaf/Usher author. [Usher syndrome is a genetic form of deaf-blindness.]

Writing it has been my biggest and toughest challenge. The story centers around the close friendship of two teenage deaf characters in an oral boarding school in England during the late 1970s, but it does sprawl out into several different strands that chronicles the entire history in relation to Deaf education, including the Milan 1880 Congress, Gallaudet University, and the Model Secondary School for the Deaf (MSSD); the suppression of sign language in Britain; and the development of auralism/oralism. Many of the characters and certain aspects of the story are based on real-life experiences by Deaf people, their families, and educationalists. The story has pretty much everything.

I spent 12 years developing the story, the last two writing the book along with extensive research. At nearly 213,000 words, it is the biggest Deaf novel ever written—12,000 more than Harlan Lane's *When the Mind Hears*, although that book is more of a historical reference book, not a novel. Although on the same subject matter of deaf education, *Innocents of Oppression* is very different from my first book. *Milan* was a fun, thrilling sci-fi fantasy adventure written in an accessible style for Deaf readers. *Innocents of Oppression* is a powerful and controversial drama with a deep, dense writing style. It can be very difficult for some to read, not because of its style, but the story itself includes some disturbing and thought-provoking storylines.

Luczak: From checking your web site, I've noticed two links: *The Limping Chicken* and *UsherLife*. Can you tell us what those sites are about?

Sturley: I'm a contributing editor for *The Limping Chicken*, which is a very popular Deaf news blog set up by Charlie Swinbourne. I write articles for it every month on a number of issues, including Usher syndrome and deafblind people. I founded *UsherLife* in 2005 as an information resource and social networking site to help people with Usher syndrome and their families in the UK to connect and share knowledge and experience. Before Facebook came along, the site had all the information such as Usher events, accessible technology product reviews, and a Yahoo egroup. It is not a support or social group, but merely an online base where people could meet "together," either virtually or socially.

Now that we have Facebook, *UsherLife* has evolved globally. The Facebook group has over 450 members worldwide. I have also encouraged many Usher people to do something positive for others such as organizing their local social meet-ups, weekend aways, and so on. It is all completely voluntary, and I run *UsherLife* with my own time and money.

Luczak: What's next on your slate? Any new projects?

Sturley: Aside from the *Tales from Signtown* and *Milan* reboots, I've no idea! Because of my Usher, which is a progressive degeneration of the retina, I don't plan ahead—I just take what it comes. However, having written and directed two short films for BSL Zone, a broadcasting and online channel for deaf programs, I plan to continue writing more scripts, and maybe even direct a few. I'm also toying with the idea of a sequel to *Innocents of Oppression*, but with a different storyline and new characters as well as some recurring characters from the first book. Although I've got the concept in mind, I still haven't been able to come up with a core story yet that would help carry the story through. We'll see.

PIA TAAVILA-BORSHEIM
Poet

When I learned about Pia Taavila-Borsheim's much-anticipated collection of poems *Moon on the Meadow*, I was naturally thrilled. As it turns out, Gallaudet University Press had never published a collection of poems by a CODA (child of Deaf adults) writer before. She was delighted to answer a few questions about her new book. She is now teaching English and creative writing at Gallaudet.

Raymond Luczak: Can you tell us a bit about your upbringing as a CODA?

Pia Taavila-Borsheim: I was the only daughter among several children, right in the middle. We kids began to use sign language from birth, as my parents would point to different toys, or a lamb on my crib, and then show us the signs for these words, as well as finger-spelling them, too, so that we'd learn the manual alphabet. I thought signing was beautiful, so animated, so passionate, so lively. I did not speak until I went to kindergarten, when I signed to my hearing teacher, "Sweater … hang where?" She probably thought I was some kind of Martian. I entered speech therapy until the fourth grade to learn how to talk and to encourage language development. Our parents almost always had the radio or the TV on, or they'd buy me a record player or an instrument to play in the school band. There was always sound, always music, but I preferred signing and would run home and cry after being made to talk in school.

Luczak: How did you get involved with poetry?

Taavila-Borsheim: In second and eighth grades, I wrote poems that made it into the school newspaper. I was thrilled to see my name in print. I had to memorize and recite poems now and then as part of my English classes, and I just fell in love with language, with how the lines broke, with the images I could envision and embrace, just by reading some well-wrought words. I'm sure a few key teachers and librarians were involved along the way. I was hooked. I began to read the great writers even while still in elementary school… Dickens, Keats, you name it. I would inhale books as a kid. You've seen the phrase "bookworm"? I was a book Anaconda.

Luczak: Do you feel that being a CODA, usually caught between two languages, has helped you as a poet?

Taavila-Borsheim: That CODA-land identity and language sword is a double-edged dagger. On one hand, having access to visual language via signing gives me a new vocabulary, a decidedly visual way of looking at the world, and certainly helps my desire to describe things so that my readers can see what I see. On the other hand, there have been times when I knew the exact sign I wanted to use in a poem, but then struggled to find the English word to match it, both in terms of meaning and nuance. I prefer signing, and yet, I'm a writer … it's a bit of a paradox.

When I give a reading of my work, I do it in several stages. First, I read the poem out loud through a microphone. I do this while an overhead transparency or a PowerPoint slide of the poem is displayed on a screen, so that the audience can read along. When I am finished verbally reading the poem, I step away from the podium, approach my audience, and then I sign the poem. But here's the crux of the dilemma: suppose I have used a word, in English, that has a possibly dual or intentionally vague meaning, and I want it that way. The moment I choose a sign for that word, I am "fixing" or setting the word's one meaning. Not too many signs include the concept of a specific word in English in all its meanings. I have to accept one sign over another, or I must significantly change the poem to include the shades of various interpretations.

For example, I once wrote a poem about my uncle, who was dying. We had all taken turns caring for him in his last days, and the poem is basically about how I am no longer afraid of death, as watching him die was actually a sacred, peaceful, blessed event, with so many loving hands helping him to pass to whatever lies on the other side. When I wrote about how thin and gaunt he'd become, I wanted to describe his hollow cheeks, my hollow heart, my grief in missing him. I used the word hollow only once, and yet it was also, in the poem, to mean the feeling I had, not just the space under his cheekbones. When I signed the poem, it was difficult to affix a sign to cover both concepts, as the words had clearly done.

Despite this, I still find that signing has helped my work rather than hindered it. I think my awareness of the richness of each language has made me a better and more visual poet, sort of like the Imagist painters.

MADAN VASISHTA
Memoirist

When *The Washington Post* reviewed Madan Vashishta's new memoir *Deaf in DC: A Memoir*, I was a bit surprised. I hadn't heard of Deaf Indians writing about their backgrounds, so I had to get in touch with the author.

Raymond Luczak: Could you please give us a summary of your background in India before you came to the United States?

Madan Vasishta: I was born in Himachal Pradesh and became deaf at the age of eleven. We lived in a village and no one, including my parents, knew what to do with me. The school I was attending let me go. So, for the next nine years I worked on our family farm, herding cattle, milking cows, plowing with oxen and so forth. However, at night I studied by myself and managed to get a high school equivalent diploma. I moved to New Delhi in 1961 to attend a photography school that was just being started for Deaf people. After finishing, I became a teacher in the same school and later took a government job as a technical photographer. I was very involved with the All India Federation of the Deaf and Delhi Deaf Association. I learned about Gallaudet through Mrs. Hester Bennet, a Deaf American traveling through India. She was in Delhi for three days and suggested I should apply to Gallaudet since I had very good English.

Luczak: How were you treated as a deaf person in India?

Vasishta: In my village, no one knew signs and neither did I. I communicated using voice and people who could write traced messages on their palm with a finger. Since they knew me as a "former hearing person," they treated me just like one of them.

In Delhi, people made fun of deaf people when they saw us signing. Deaf people were—still are at times—ridiculed. I couldn't complain much, however. I got a very good job with the government. Opportunities for most Deaf people were very limited. Most of them depended on their families as there was no government support system. Even now, the situation has not improved much. Today only five to ten percent Deaf children go to school.

I work in India for two or three months each year as a volunteer trainer and consultant, and am impressed with the progress being made there now. A law (Persons with Disabilities Act), based on the U.S. Americans with Disabilities

Act, was passed in 1993 in India. However, it is not implemented very well. India ratified the UNCRPD, and this might help change things, albeit slowly.

Luczak: Do you think that racism and prejudice still exists for Deaf Indians within the American Deaf community?

Vasishta: It is hard to say. When I was at Gallaudet, I forgot I was from India. No one ever let me feel I was different and treated me differently. However, racism does exist. It is a part of human nature. It is shrouded, however. I never felt being discriminated at any stage. A Deaf person from India becoming a superintendent of two different schools shows that America is still the land of opportunity. Still, when I finished my Ph.D., I did not get any job offer. Those days, very few Deaf people had the terminal degree and anyone getting Ph.D.s got a plum good job and fast. My applications were either ignored or rejected. One administrator at Gallaudet called three school superintendents asking them why I was not being considered for the jobs I had applied for. One response was: "You want me to hire someone whose name I cannot even spell?" Later, after the Deaf President Now movement, hiring Deaf people as administrators became more common.

Luczak: Today many people are encouraged to reclaim their original ethnic identities. How is it different now?

Vasishta: We are more aware of diversity and encourage hiring and involvement of people from minority groups. However, what they did back in the 70s and 80s came more from the heart. Today it is enforced by laws and, I hate to say it, it has become a fad. At times, when people say things like "Diversity is beautiful," it sounds fake. It is just like how many hearing people say, "Deaf people are cute!" Oh, no!

Luczak: Do you celebrate the Indian part of your identity and if so, what do you do to celebrate?

Vasishta: I was the only Indian at Gallaudet for six years. Even my name sign was a thumb going up in the middle of the forehead or "the" Indian. However, I was fully mainstreamed into the regular Gallaudet crowd. Now that many Deaf people from India live in the U.S., it is a different story. I do associate with other Deaf people from India and Asia, and we celebrate the Hindu and Muslim new years under an organization called Metro South Asian Deaf Association.

ROSA LEE TIMM
Poet and Performer

When I first learned about Rosa Lee Timm's new poetry collection *Bathlight*, I was excited. The book looked beautiful!

Raymond Luczak: Where did you go to school?

Rosa Lee Timm: My mother had wanted to become a teacher long before my brothers and I were born so we were her first students. She taught us from pre-school to second grade before enrolling us in a private school. We were the only deaf students out of over 100 plus hearing students so we was taught mainly via sign language interpreters and the FM system. We eventually transferred to Indiana School for the Deaf where we received a bilingual/bicultural education.

Luczak: It appears that you come from a Deaf family. What were your impressions of hearing families while growing up?

Timm: Come to think of it, my childhood friends were also children of Deaf parents. I don't think I was fully exposed to a hearing family until I was ten years old. I befriended a classmate of mine who often invited me over to her place. She got a huge trampoline in her backyard so I couldn't resist. Her family was hearing and that time turned out to be incredibly frustrating. Nobody seemed to care what everybody was doing or where they were going. I was so accustomed to knowing everybody's business and I would often ask my friend where her sister was going or what her siblings were talking about. She would simply shrug and say, "I don't know," as if it was no big deal.

Luczak: How did you get involved with performing onstage?

Timm: Youth Leadership Camp was where it all started. Naturally, I had done some plays at home and at a church before that, but I never felt as inspired as I did at that camp. Mark Wood was my drama teacher at YLC during the summer of 1991. He told the most amazing ASL stories I have ever saw. I felt inspired to test my waters as a performer and I've never looked back since.

Luczak: Why do you write?

Timm: My family are mostly writers. My father is probably the one who started it all. Both of my brothers have degrees in English and creative writing; they have written novels and poetry for as long as I have known them. My older brother is currently an English teacher at California State University in

Northridge, and my younger brother, a graduate student at Johns Hopkins University, is studying poetry. My mother also wrote poetry during her high school years, and some of her work was published in a local newspaper. I write because it felt natural to do so. I wrote a lot during college after meeting other Deaf poets and have found it quite therapeutic. These are the reasons why I write.

Luczak: Tell us a bit about your new book *Bathlight*. Why that title?

Timm: My new book is a collection of selected poems of mine that I wrote during college. They are mainly about love and the drama that comes with it. I chose to call it *Bathlight* because I do my best thinking while taking a candlelit bath. *Bathlight* seemed like a fitting title.

MICHAEL NORTHEN
Editor and Reviewer

When it comes to the arts, many people are always interested in what critics think. Michael Northen, who edits material and reviews books for *Wordgathering*, a web site geared toward promoting disability and Deaf literature, intrigued me because he's always given my books the most insightful reviews from a disability literature viewpoint. (For the record, he doesn't love everything I've written, but he is certainly one of the most thoughtful critics out there!)

Raymond Luczak: How did you get involved with the disability community?

Michael Northen: I became involved in with the disability community when, after almost thirty years as an educator, I came to work at Inglis House, a wheelchair community, in Philadelphia. I don't have a disability myself, but I had worked with prisoners, children in inner-city Camden, and women on public assistance. I was also a group home parent for abused and pre-delinquent children, and a learning disabilities resource room teacher in rural Georgia, so I did have a fair amount of experience in working with people who were not exactly mainstream.

When I arrived at Inglis House, some of the residents there heard that I wrote poetry and asked if we could form a group and, thus, the Inglis House poetry workshop was born. At first we discussed our own work and produced chapbooks of our work. At the same time, though, we wanted to connect with the poetry of others who had disabilities to see how our poetry could grow. We really dismayed at the lack of what seemed to be available and so in 2003 began the Inglis House Poetry Contest, which became an annual event. We also began publishing an annual chapbook. It allowed us to see what was happening in disability poetry. One year we even ran an all-day conference on disability and poetry at Inglis House.

On a more personal note, I had returned to school to work on my doctorate after a 30-year hiatus, and I wrote my dissertation on the developing field of disability literature.

Luczak: What prompted you to set up *Wordgathering*?

Northen: *Wordgathering* was an outgrowth of the Inglis House Poetry

Workshop and its annual contest. We had developed a website for the group's poetry previously, but wanted to do something that would promote the work of other writers with disability. Moreover, we saw how cliché-ridden, patronizing, and sentimental most poetry about disability was and wanted to counter that. Unfortunately, Inglis House has only a few Deaf residents, so there is not a real sense of a Deaf community here. Moreover, those who are deaf also tend to have additional conditions such as cerebral palsy that makes using ASL especially difficult. The first year of our contest, one deaf resident submitted a poem about her loneliness and isolation. It was not a great poem, but the sense of alienation from others that it conveyed really struck me. It is also a frustrating experience for some of the residents who have a real interest in ASL and yet they do not have the fine motor coordination to be able to sign themselves.

Working with *Wordgathering* has helped me get to more about the Deaf community of which, I admit, I was totally ignorant when I first came to Inglis House. One work that especially influenced me was John Lee Clark's *Deaf American Poetry*. It got me to know the work of Curtis Robbins, Christopher Jon Heuer, and John's own work. Another work that really made an impression on me was your book *Whispers of a Savage Sort and Other Plays about the Deaf American Experience*. The dynamics within the Deaf community that your plays portrayed really changed my view of Deaf culture, which I had naïvely thought to be much more harmonious. With *Wordgathering*, I also had a chance to learn about the work of the Deaf artist Betty G. Miller, whose paintings are simply wonderful. Frankly, the stereotypes about disability still abound in the submissions that we receive, but things are definitely changing for the better.

Luczak: How did your anthology *Beauty is a Verb: The New Poetry of Disability* come about?

Northen: *Beauty is a Verb* came about as a result of a panel at the 2010 Associated Writers Program conference in Denver. Sheila Black, whose poetry I admire greatly, asked me to participate along with several other poets in a panel about poetry and disability, focusing on perceptions of people with disabilities. (Ellen Smith, who is becoming increasingly deaf, titled her portion of the talk "Hearing A Pear.") For a long time I had seen the need for an anthology that represent quality poetry by writers with physical disabilities. Just go to your local bookstore—you won't find one there. So I mentioned this to Sheila.

Immediately after the conference, I had to have open-heart surgery. When I returned from the hospital, Sheila sent me an email, saying that she and another panel member, Jennifer Bartlett, had formulated the idea for the book and asked if I wanted to be in on it.

Editing *Beauty is a Verb* has been an extremely interesting and intense experience. Each of us comes from a very different background. One of the ironies in our debates is that while I am the only editor without a disability (and thus my poetry cannot even appear in the book), I am the one who has lobbied hardest to get representative from the Disabilities Studies movement like Jim Ferris and Stephen Kuusisto as well as some of the excellent but relatively unknown poets that I have met through *Wordgathering* included. Sheila and Jen, on the other hand, are a lot more sophisticated and knowledgeable about contemporary poetry than I am. We all agree that without any one of us it could not be the same book, but all signs are that we have a real winner here.

MORGAN GRAYCE WILLOW
Poet

Morgan Grayce Willow first attracted my attention some years ago when her book *Crossing That Bridge: A Guide to Making Literary Events Accessible to the Deaf and Hard of Hearing* came out. Then I learned of her new chapbook *Arpeggio of Appetite*.

Raymond Luczak: How did you become involved with the signing community?

Morgan Grayce Willow: I met the Deaf actress Marian Lucas, and we teamed up on a project in which Marian translated and performed my poems. At that time I knew very few signs. We communicated primarily by writing notes, with occasional help from volunteer interpreters. We used lots of gesture and mime, which pushed me, as a shy, hearing person, beyond my comfort zone. The show was a success. Then, I wanted to do more collaborative work with Marian and other Deaf artists, so I started studying ASL—first with Northern Sign Theater, a Deaf company then active in Minneapolis, later at Saint Paul College. After level three, I felt I still hadn't learned enough, so I entered the Interpreter Training Program. Eventually, I left interpreting to return to teaching; however, my relationship with the signing community continues.

Luczak: What prompted you to write *Crossing That Bridge*?

Willow: I had been writing poetry for many years before becoming an interpreter. I was shocked to discover how many interpreters feared interpreting poetry. During graduate school, we'd studied great poets from other cultures and languages, in translation. I don't know, for example, where I would be without Rilke. Though I knew some German, I was not competent to translate his poems. We struggled with the notion of a successful translation. So I came to ASL poetry—which I couldn't access without interpreters—with an open mind.

I wrote *Crossing That Bridge* to facilitate exchange between audiences and poets on both sides of the hearing/signing, English/ASL border. One of the issues I had to address was a general reluctance among interpreters—most of whom were not literature majors, much less poets—to approach the task of interpreting poetry. I also addressed the overall ignorance in the literary community about how to make public poetry readings accessible to Deaf/Hard-of-Hearing audiences. Most had never worked with an interpreter. The book details these logistics in a step-by-step way that makes it easy for organizers. It also emphasizes how to work directly with Deaf artists and poets.

Luczak: Do you think your knowledge of ASL has had any impact on your poetry?

Willow: I always strive to make my poems visual through imagery—to find images that bring together an "emotional and intellectual complex in an instant of time," to borrow from Ezra Pound. This is best achieved with concrete language, specific detail expressed in precise terms, which then blossoms into universal human experience. This happens in both ASL and English poetry.

I've certainly learned about space in language from ASL. In English poems, space occurs in the combinations of specific sounds and rhythms as they shift and fall from line to line. In ASL poetry, the use of visual space is heightened to maximum artistic effect. Maybe it would be accurate to say that I "feel" space in both an auditory and a visual way, which may not have been true in the same way had I not learned ASL.

For some time, I struggled to write a poem about ASL poetry. This occurred well before I had actually seen much ASL poetry. One day, a writer friend introduced me to the pantoum. At first I dismissed the form as convoluted and archaic, but I soon discovered that its pattern of repeated lines gave me precisely the form I needed to say something about the repetition of movement and shape in ASL poetry. The poem that emerged, "Sign is an Anagram of Sing," appeared in *The Tactile Mind*.

Luczak: How did *Arpeggio of Appetite* come out?

Willow: The chapbook emerged from experiments with form. I don't recall when I first discovered the cinquain—a five-line, twenty-two syllable form that resembles, in some ways, haiku and tanka. I began to write a cinquain each morning as an exercise in sharpening my skill with imagery and economy of language. Then one day I was packing for a writing retreat in Puget Sound. I knew it would be a beautiful setting; I also knew that my photography skills would be woefully inadequate for capturing that beauty. I decided to write an album of cinquains instead. Years later, I collected the very best from among the hundreds of cinquains I'd written to shape a chapbook. That became *Arpeggio of Appetite*.

SHARON PAJKA
Blogger

When I visited Gallaudet University recently, I had the good fortune of meeting Sharon Pajka, who's been blogging about Deaf characters in Young Adult (YA) literature for a while now. Considering how books can help young deaf people, particularly if they're not in a Deaf-positive environment, I felt that her blog was too important to ignore.

Raymond Luczak: When you meet a Deaf person who doesn't know anything about you or your educational background, what do you normally say?

Sharon Pajka: I have Meniere's disease (vertigo, ears ringing, and fluctuating hearing loss). My mother suggested taking an ASL class just in case I fully lost my hearing, as the doctors had warned. Our instructor, Deaf himself, was a Gallaudet graduate. When we initially started the class, my mom and I wanted to walk out, thinking there was no possible way we could learn the language. We were both very nervous about not being able to communicate with our teacher. After study and practice, I still remember the first real conversation that I had with my instructor. It wasn't about homework or the weather; it wasn't about anything that we studied in class per se, but we were chatting during a break when he stopped me smiling and signed, "See, we understand each other." That was my breakthrough moment when I thought, "Hey, this foreign language stuff isn't so bad." Learning a second language really just helped me reflect upon my first language. In that sense, ASL helped me like English more.

I'm asked a great deal of questions. On campus when someone meets me and I say I live in Richmond, VA (that's right, 120 miles south) and that my daily commute round trip is six hours (three hours each way), my sanity is questioned more than anything else. One of the courses that I teach is in the General Studies program, and its focus is about the meaning and importance of "place." Space + meaning = Place. I love Richmond, and I love Gallaudet.

Luczak: How did you fall into teaching English literature?

Pajka: I double-majored in English and Religious Studies with a focus on World Cultures in undergrad and that I have always been fascinated with culture in general, but I never wanted to become a teacher. However, as I was taking

ASL, my instructor encouraged me to attend graduate school. I always knew I wanted to go back to school, but had no idea what I wanted to do. I'm still not sure why I applied to the Education Department. I guess he said he thought I'd be good and I thought, "Well, okay." Once I was actually with teens during my first internship, I discovered this was my calling. I love working with young adults—the snarkier, the better.

Luczak: How did your blog on Deaf YA characters come about?

Pajka: I was teaching a High School English course at a residential school for the Deaf and one of my students requested summer reading. She challenged me with the stipulation that the book recommendation had to include characters similar to her and her peers. Since that time, I have been collecting and reviewing books with deaf characters. In 2006, I completed my doctoral dissertation, The portrayals and perceptions of deaf characters in adolescent literature, and began an educational blog, *Deaf Characters in Adolescent Literature*. My initial goal for the blog was to have a place to compile details from my research, to list books with deaf characters, and to recommend books to all the students out in cyberspace who were seeking characters similar to themselves. I never planned for the blog to grow as large as it has. The blog now includes more than 30 author interviews and a list of 200+ books with deaf characters ranging from younger adolescents who read juvenile chapter books to crossover adult books that include young adult deaf characters.

When I meet a Deaf character, I'm usually looking for how that character is portrayed. Is he or she realistic? Has the author included more than one deaf character? Who is the intended audience? Is the factual information correct? Is it a cultural or a pathological perception of Deaf people? In my dissertation, I developed a Content-Analysis Check-Off form so that I can go through and see which aspects are more cultural or pathologically portrayed.

Luczak: In your humble opinion, what do you consider to be the most realistically-drawn Deaf YA character, and why?

Pajka: Jacqueline Woodson's characters in *Feathers* struggle to find balance in a world of racial segregation and living on the "other side" of the tracks. Her character Sean, who is the first Deaf African-American character I have found in adolescent literature who uses sign language and attends a deaf school, tries to find his way as an adolescent in a world where he is discriminated against based on his skin color, deafness, and residence. The book is about "hope," not deafness or isolation.

Jean Ferris includes all deaf characters except the hearing son Theo and another CODA named Ivy in *Of Sound Mind*. Theo is embarrassed by his parents not because they're deaf but because he is a teenager and he feels different. I think most teens can relate to that. While reading the book, I wanted to be Ivy. She was so cool. Interestingly enough, the character's deaf father is the first Deaf character I've found with a Ph.D. in adolescent literature. Now there are many great Deaf role models for young people.

One of my favorite books has a secondary deaf character. Paul Rowe used his mother's experiences in his novel *The Silent Time* which has a strong sense of place in Newfoundland and a compelling plot that reads much like a play (not surprisingly since Rowe is both an actor and playwright). I was emotionally invested in each of the characters. With that being said, it is hard to believe that this is the author's debut novel.

Luczak: What are some of the best YA titles for readers interested in Deaf characters?

Pajka: My list would have to include these titles: *Feathers*, Jacqueline Woodson; *The Silent Time*, Paul Rowe; *Five Flavors of Dumb*, Antony John; *The Dark Days of Hamburger Halpin*, Josh Berk; *Of Sound Mind*, Jean Ferris; *T4*, Ann Clare LeZotte; *Leading Ladies*, Marlee Matlin and Doug Cooney; *Singing Hands*, Delia Ray; and *The Sign for Drowning*, Rachel Stolzman. I have more than 200 titles on my blog.

DAVE GALANTER
Science Fiction Novelist

It has been over twenty years since Howie Seago, one of our esteemed Deaf actors, appeared on the TV program *Star Trek: The Next Generation*, so when I heard about the hearing author Dave Galanter's novel *Troublesome Minds* using characters who didn't speak in the *Star Trek* universe, I was very intrigued.

Raymond Luczak: What was your childhood like?

Dave Galanter: Average, I suppose. I grew up in Michigan, to older parents so even though I'm generation X, I think I have some baby-boomer qualities sometimes. I went to school in Flint, Michigan, and to college at Michigan State University with a degree in Journalism, which I've not much used. I was always close with my parents, and while my mom passed away, I'm still very close with my father and talk with him daily.

Luczak: What kind of books did you enjoy reading?

Galanter: I like both science fiction and mystery novels, and sadly my favorite author just passed away. Robert B. Parker, author of the Spenser and Jesse Stone detective novels. It's very sad to think I won't be able to enjoy new adventures from this man's mind. But at least I have the old books to reread and cherish. I think he's my favorite author because his prose style is so easy to read. He achieves something I strive for when I write, which is a very conversational tone, as if someone was sitting, telling me a story. I try to write like that, as best I can.

Luczak: How did you end up working at Gallaudet University?

Galanter: I didn't like my job in Michigan, and Michigan didn't have a lot of jobs, so I decided to move to the D.C. area. Because I could sign, I checked Gallaudet's website to see if they had any job openings in the Information Technology department, and they did. I was rather surprised when I got the invitation to interview, because I honestly figured there would be a Gallaudet graduate who would apply for the position, but one did not, and I guess I was the only person to have applied who had the experience they were looking for, and that I happened to sign as well was a bonus. (I didn't really consider my signing that great, since I'd never signed in a professional environment before, and it is different than signing casually, but I've learned a great deal just by working every day.)

Luczak: How did you end up writing books on the side?

Galanter: I'd always wanted to be a writer, but I didn't like the instability of that career. You don't have a weekly paycheck or benefits, and I wanted those things, so I decided to write what I could, when I could, on the side. When I was in college, I had some friends who wrote professionally, and they took me under their wing and helped me get started.

Luczak: The premise of your book *Troublesome Minds* sounds intriguing. Where did you find its inspiration?

Galanter: The book is really a story of three people's loneliness. One is the *Star Trek* character people know—Spock—and two are from a telepathic race called the Isitri. In creating this telepathic race, I wanted to explore how such a race would be. If they didn't need to talk, perhaps they wouldn't develop vocal chords and so wouldn't be able to speak at all. And so, how would they communicate with those who were disabled in their own community (meaning those who lacked the telepathic ability)? Well, it seemed natural that they'd develop a manual language. I also thought since their communication didn't depend on hearing, they might have a high number of deaf people (I suggested they might have up to one-third deaf). This allowed me to explore a couple of different things: how those with manual language can communicate technologically, and also what it would mean to be able to so easily communicate with others—via thought—and how might one be isolated without that ability. Part of the inspiration for all that was that I'd always wanted to write a deaf main character, as well as use sign language in a book.

Luczak: What's next for you?

Galanter: I don't know. I have an episode of a *Star Trek* Internet web show that I co-wrote that will be out this spring, and I have some feelers out to write some more *Star Trek* books perhaps, but I'm also trying to find time to get a social life going, so I'm trying to write a bit less and enjoy life a bit more.

LINDA DRATELL
Writer and Editor

I'd first heard of the editor Linda Dratell when she informed me that a few of my poems would appear in *The 2011 ALDA Reader*, a magazine that would be distributed by the Association of Late-Deafened Adults (ALDA) at their convention.

Raymond Luczak: Within the Deaf and/or signing and/or hearing loss communities, how do you identify yourself?

Linda Dratell: I identify myself as late-deafened, as it gives others in the community a sense of my background in comparison to theirs. I had lost my hearing in my 30s, after finishing college and graduate school, marrying and adopting my first child.

Luczak: How did you get involved with ALDA?

Dratell: I had just lost much of my hearing, and my audiologist recommended that I attend a support group. I met a woman who, at the time, was the president of the local ALDA chapter. I had never met anyone else who was deafened like me before, and there she was, elegant and poised, and because of her own wonderful self-esteem I knew finally that I would be okay. She invited me to my first ALDA meeting.

At my first ALDA meeting there were so many people who were late-deafened, I couldn't believe it. I started crying, really out of relief to find soul mates. Several women crowded around me, and one said, "Why are you crying, we are your family!" I will never forget that. I am still friends with these same individuals. I feel indebted to ALDA. I can't do enough to give back to the organization that helped me become whole again. I became Region 4 (Western Region) Director, then President last year. This year is my last year on the board as Past President.

Luczak: Were you always a writer?

Dratell: I have always enjoyed writing, but have only had a few articles published since my hearing loss. I used to try my hand at fiction, but writing about losing my hearing and learning sign language has been a wonderful experience and outlet for me. I have always enjoyed creating stories, ever since I was young. Later, when I attended a class in Deaf Culture, I wrote a paper about my own journey through hearing loss and it was later published. I felt cleansed through my writing and wrote more articles. Also, poetry was always important to my parents, and they shared that love of the written word with me. We would memorize poems together, such as "Paul Revere's Ride." I enjoy persuasive writing, expressing experiences that others can relate to that compel people to action.

Luczak: You're editing your first *ALDA Reader*. What has the experience been like for you so far?

Dratell: It's interesting to be on the other side of the acceptance/rejection letter! I finally understand what goes into putting a collection of works together. I've learned for myself that editing is an art as well as writing. The end product, the collection of works, is something you mold and form just like you would a story. It's a fascinating process, one that is very fulfilling. I have had help from two experienced editors, as well as a lot of material submitted. I believe the variety of material submitted really represents the array of experiences from our community. We can hold up this publication and say, "This is us."

RACHEL C. MAZIQUE
Scholar

When I learned about the focus of Rachel's studies for her Ph.D. while as part of our Deaf Artists Residency Program at the Anderson Center for Interdisciplinary Arts in Red Wing, Minnesota, I had to ask her more.

Raymond Luczak: Can you please give us a quick recap of your background?

Rachel C. Mazique: I'm part of the third generation of Deaf people in my family; after graduating from John Hersey High School in Illinois, I went on to major in Deaf Education at Flagler College. When I transferred to Gallaudet University, I double-majored in English and Education with a minor in Psychology. After a summer abroad learning Spanish Sign Language (LSE) and British Sign Language (BSL), I started graduate school at the University of Texas at Austin. I completed my Masters in English in 2010, and I'm currently a Ph.D. Candidate in English. Broadly, my dissertation examines how literature can promote social justice; I'm working with transatlantic Deaf literature (from both the UK and the US).

Luczak: Were you always a reader?

Mazique: Yes, I started reading before kindergarten. My mom would sign the words in books, and I became fascinated with the printed word and would read everything around me. My parents provided a print-rich environment—from the menus at the kitchen table, to cereal boxes, to all the books in the floor-to-ceiling bookshelves taking up an entire wall, the captions on the TV, visits to the library and the library mobile, billboards and signs when out on the road—I was always seeing what words I could read and understand. In kindergarten, I was one of the best readers in class while others struggled to read aloud. I loved reading books that were part of serials. Stand-alone novels ended too soon. I liked stories that never ended because they were part of long children's serials—such as *The Boxcar Children*. Those mysteries probably prompted my lifelong love of mysteries. I later liked to read mystery books by Caroline B. Cooney and remember giving a presentation on her thriller *Emergency Room*. *The Man who Loved Clowns* was also an early favorite. Stories about diverse people always appealed to me—whether it was about a man with Down's syndrome, Amish people, or people in and out of the hospital living with life-threatening illnesses. Thanks to my parents, I was a baby bookworm.

Luczak: Who was the first Deaf character in literature that left an impact on you?

Mazique: I don't remember reading of any Deaf fictional character as a child. I think my first encounter with a deaf character in literature occurred in high school when we read *The Adventures of Huckleberry Finn*, but no one talked about the duke impersonating a deaf person and Twain's caricature of deaf people. No one talked about Jim's "poor" deaf daughter. I believe I read that book before I had interpreters in the classroom, and before I had interpreters, I was more of a "listener" than a speaker. I was always afraid to say something that others had already said, but that I didn't hear. I didn't want to make a fool of myself by repeating what someone else said. So I never brought up those minor characters either. I didn't know what to do with them and simply "listened" to whatever the teacher said. From what I remember, most of the discussion centered on race and the use of the "n" word as well as how some schools censored or banned the book from their libraries and classrooms. It was not until I was in graduate school and doing my own research that I came across Christopher Krentz's article "Exploring the 'Hearing Line': Deafness, Laughter and Mark Twain." When I read it, I felt like my high school discussion on the novel was finally "complete" because here was a perspective that brought much insight to a novel and an author by closely analyzing the roles of these minor/supporting characters in the novel. I suppose, indirectly, through Krentz's article, Twain's novel, and his deaf characters are the first that left an impact on me because Krentz taught me how these seemingly insignificant characters are quite significant when considering the historical context of the novel as well as the biographical content of Twain's life.

Luczak: What made you realize that you wanted to become a teacher of literature?

Mazique: I've always loved reading, but in second grade I realized I wanted to become a teacher. My second-grade teacher made learning a lot of fun, and I wanted to be like him. In high school, I decided I wanted to teach at the high school level, and my favorite subject was English. It was also in high school that I realized I would most enjoy teaching Deaf students. I worked in the Writing Lab tutoring anyone who wanted help with their papers. I remember giving writing advice to seniors as a sophomore Honors English student. I mostly tutored hearing students since John Hersey is a mainstream school.

Once Deaf students realized I worked there, some of them came to see me. These students had become my friends since high school was the first time I was among Deaf peers. They were also the most appreciative of my writing advice and explanations; they said they felt like they understood more from me than from their teachers. Their input had a huge impact on me and made me feel like I knew where I belonged and would belong as a teacher. At Gallaudet University, my advisor and one of my English professors, Dr. Jill Bradbury, said I belonged in graduate school. She was right, and I love teaching at the University of Texas, but I do still hope to have the opportunity to teach D/deaf as well as hearing college students.

Luczak: What are some of the things you've learned from teaching your students? Do you think that as a Deaf teacher, you find cultural expectations differing between hearing and Deaf students? How so?

Mazique: I've never had a Deaf college student, but I did have one deaf student who didn't know any sign language. And because my literature course had a Deaf Studies component, it meant a lot when she wrote that she felt like she had a greater appreciation of who she was as a deaf person as well as of ASL and Deaf culture.

My students are often taken aback when they realize their instructor is Deaf and will be teaching them how to become better readers, writers and thinkers (in English) even though I'm communicating with them in a different language (ASL). Although they're taken aback and some even consider dropping my class because I'm Deaf, those who stick around have taught me the value of Deaf Studies in the classroom. These students are most appreciative of the knowledge they gain about language, communication, difference, and diversity in cultural perspectives.

Luczak: Likewise, did you come across bias in the work you analyzed?

Mazique: All works are biased, and bias in and of itself is not a bad thing. The problem with biased works comes about when it's a canonical problem of oversight or unbalanced perspectives that are not in conversation with differing perspectives. My job is to present the range of perspectives and to talk about the significant historical/contemporary contexts—contexts that speak to human rights issues—as well as the cognitive effects of reading stereotypical representations of the Deaf experience/deafness in contrast to more realistic or unique representations of Sign Language Peoples.

Luczak: In Red Wing, you were introduced as a "scholar." What does it mean to you, personally, to be a scholar?

Mazique: My graduate education has trained me in the scholarly enterprise of reading, interrogating, discussing, and writing academic works. To me, being a scholar means we are skilled in the craft of close reading, analysis, critique, and synthesis. My passion lies in teaching, and I see my work as a scholar as closely linked to my drive to educate. Scholarly work is about researching, reading, and then writing in order to bring our insights to particular audiences. In the end, it's all about teaching, educating, and encouraging conversation—even arguments. As a scholar in the humanities, I'm motivated by work that strives to educate in order to bring about cognitive-emotional interactions that can impact social policies and create a more just world.

Luczak: How do you think your scholarship would help the Deaf community, or the cause for more in-depth analysis of Deaf-related writing?

Mazique: It's my hope that my scholarship will contribute to the growing interest in Deaf literature—that teachers, instructors, professors, parents and librarians will read, purchase, and bring works of Deaf literature into their classrooms, homes and libraries in order to foster conversation about Sign Language Peoples (SLPs) as an ethnic group. Such an education would encourage a rethinking of the human rights of SLPs and promote the protection of sign language, Deaf culture, and Deaf lives. I believe that through reading a range of Deaf literature and an education in Deaf studies, parents who learn that their child may be deaf will be less likely to feel that this is cause for abortion. Although there will always be people who seek to hear like they once could or to have their child hear as they can, perhaps more people will seek to learn a new language or to cherish the native signed language of their people rather than seek or feel compelled to seek a "cure." Understanding the value and benefits in preserving and protecting SLPs can lead to a flourishing of Deaf art, visual media and businesses that benefit both hearing and deaf people, sign language literature, sign language performances, and signed languages themselves.

RUSSELL KANE
Novelist

When I heard that Russell Kane's novel *Fighting the Long Sorrow: A Journey to Personhood* had scenes from the Deaf President Now (DPN) movement, my interest was piqued, particularly since I had participated in DPN.

Raymond Luczak: Could you tell us a bit about your background?

Russell Kane: I was born profoundly deaf because my mother had rubella in her first trimester. I was raised orally in New York and my mother used the John Tracy Clinic correspondence course with me when she quit her high school English teaching career to stay home with me.

My father was in medical school at that time as a resident so he was out a lot working. When my father finished school, he was in the Air Force and we lived near Central Institute for the Deaf in St. Louis. When he was done with the USAF, we moved back to New York to be near family. I attended the Lexington School for the Deaf in first and second grades.

Then we moved again, this time to Suffolk County. That January, I tried a four-month experiment at a public school near us to see if I could handle the academic structure of a mainstream school. It was deemed a success so when we moved, I went to mainstream schools all the way up to my high school graduation. I was a very good student with all As and Bs. But I had no friends. I never dated in my four years of high school.

My family did not sign even though my sisters did fingerspell. I was left out of all dinner conversations so when I became a teenager, I rebelled against the rule that nobody could leave the table until everyone was finished. My attitude was that if I couldn't understand the dialogue happening around me, I was "exempt" from this rule.

I still do not usually attend family events because of the communication difficulties. However, if I have someone to go with me, I will be more open to attending these events because I won't feel alone. Hearing people don't realize how tough lipreading is. The best lipreaders catch only 30% of what is visible on the lips. The rest is contextual, filling in the blanks, and guesswork.

A favorite childhood story of mine deals with my other sister, Beth. Every time I bothered her, punched her, or annoyed her, my mother would tell me,

"Go polish her eyes!" Of course, I was very confused and puzzled about how I was supposed to polish someone's eyes, but to placate her I went to Beth and said, "I polish your eyes." Then Beth would appear satisfied and walk away. This happened repeatedly until I was about ten years old. One day when I was reading, I came across the word "apologize"—only then did I realize what I had been saying all along!

Luczak: What was Gallaudet like?

Kane: Gallaudet, what a totally different world. I remember the first time I ever visited with my parents as a high school junior in 1981 checking out colleges. Entering the Ely Student Center, I gasped at all of the Deaf people there signing at the same time. It overwhelmed me, as I had just started learning sign language through two deaf friends of mine who lived near me.

But I decided to go to the Rochester Institute of Technology (RIT), as it had over 1,000 Deaf students right there at NTID. But I transferred out and then I graduated from Hofstra University in 1986. Two years later I decided to go back to Gallaudet as a graduate student. By this time, I was fluent in signing, but not in ASL, so I felt confident I would be fine this time around.

I had the most amazing two and a half years of my life at Gallaudet first as a special undergraduate student in the spring of 1988 and then as a graduate student for two years. I happened to be there during Deaf President Now (DPN) and I would not trade this experience for anything. Imagine, after just two months on campus, I was thrown into a maelstrom of controversy, activism, and emotions! That week changed my entire life and the direction I would eventually take. It is a major reason why I am now an ASL professor at Nassau Community College. I want to affect the perspective of hearing people and how they see Deaf culture and history along with ASL.

Gallaudet was the "total experience" with not only academics but also social learning. I was exposed to new life experiences including my first-ever girlfriend who was Deaf herself. I had never experienced a romantic relationship, and at age 24, I was about to learn. I made many new friendships that I had never really had before on a college campus. All of the hearing students at Gallaudet signed so that was something I had never seen at RIT or Hofstra. I felt like I belonged, finally. Never before in my life did I feel "normal" and just a "face in the crowd." Gallaudet was similar to the show *Cheers* when everyone knew each other in that bar in Boston.

Luczak: What sort of things have you learned from teaching ASL to hearing students?

Kane: I have seen things and read papers that I didn't think were possible out there. At the beginning of the semester, I give out a true-false quiz to my ASL 152 (Level 1) students to gauge their understanding of Deaf culture and ASL. Some surprising things that I've seen them say are: deaf people can't drive, deaf people read Braille, deaf people cannot marry other deaf people, ASL is the same language as English, ASL is universal all over the world, Thomas Gallaudet himself was a deaf person (this is understandable), oral/auditory use helps a student learn ASL better (known as simultaneous communication), and many other misconceptions.

Luczak: How did *Fighting the Long Sorrow* come about?

Kane: I was feeling a lot of frustration with my family in the summer of 2010 because of a recent experience with my nieces and nephews. They came up to me, happy that I had come to a family event, and started talking to me. I was unable to understand a single word they said, so they were unhappy and so was I. On top of that, I felt it was very unfair for me to be excluded from what was happening around me with family at Thanksgiving, Passover, Chanukah, and parties.

Up to that point, I had refused to go on several family vacations to resorts and on cruises. I could not imagine spending a week with the people who loved me the most. I know that is hard for many hearing people to imagine, but it is a common experience among Deaf people. I see that "knowing nod" among Deaf people in an audience when I recount this experience and at the same time, I see bewilderment on hearing people's faces because they have never experienced this. When the hearing students start going to Deaf events, they start to get an idea of what Deaf people like me have gone through, feeling like a foreigner in a different land, being unable to understand what is happening around them.

Since the book came out, I have felt much more positive about myself. Seeing positive comments from Deaf people, my ASL students, and the public has really inspired me even more to write another novel. I remember my mother's 70th birthday party last December in Florida. I was very skeptical about coming down for the party until my parents told me they wanted an interpreter there! I was very touched about this and felt a lot better.

When I went down there, I saw my good friend Reed, his wife and kids, and all of my family and my parents' friends. They were very excited about my book and I felt like the man of the hour. The interpreter made all the difference. I even got to see my cousin Herb who has since then passed away. He and I were close when I attended Hofstra, and I was so happy I got to see him one more time. I had so much fun at the party and my family got to see me for whom I really am: a person! I have always imagined what it would be like to have a family who signed all the time around me. I have no doubt I would be such a different person, happier, more outgoing, and content.

JENNIFER DANS-WILLEY
Editor

When I learned that the newspaper *SIGNews* would be put on hiatus after nine years, I insisted on giving Jennifer Dans-Willey, its Editor-in-Chief, the same treatment I'd given my subjects before her last day on the job.

Raymond Luczak: Tell us a bit about your background. Were you always Deaf?

Jennifer Dans-Willey: I was born in London, Ontario, Canada. I was definitely blessed to have been born to deaf parents. Deaf at birth, I naturally learned how to sign "milk" at eight months old. I have two Deaf brothers and a Deaf sister all spread out in two countries. My oldest brother resides in Winnipeg, Canada; my younger brother lives in Chicago, and my sister lives in Riverside, California.

Luczak: Was reading always a part of your life?

Dans-Willey: Reading wasn't my favorite thing to do, to be honest. I was a theater kid. I loved to play shows; I loved to do stand up for my family. I love to make everyone laugh. At 12 years old, I really started to understand stories. My homeroom/reading/writing teacher thought that being around computers would help students read and write more. It was the Commodore 64 with this huge floppy disk drive that helped me read. That teacher taught all of my siblings. We all read because of this man. We all are successful because of this man. We all still keep in touch with Mr. Ron Foster, a hearing teacher who had absolute passion to teach reading, writing, and imagination through computers, via Facebook. He still beams with pride when he sees us students chatting up a storm via social media! To this day, I smile when I read a book. I have instilled the love for reading to my sons, starting them way earlier than myself.

Luczak: How did you become interested in the writing business? What was your experience prior to joining *SIGNews*?

Dans-Willey: You will laugh at this. Zilch. I joined up as the news editor when David Rosenbaum was the Editor-in-Chief (EIC). I was well-known for establishing a system and running with it, cleaning up, getting things organized, on track, etc. At that time in 2006, *SIGNews* was experiencing severe shortage with staff along with a severe shortage of money, ending up being three months behind with its distribution. Within three months, I managed to get five issues out and get back on track mid-month at one month and back on track, distributing at the first week of month ever since. I started to learn how to write that time. I learned how to edit. I learned on the job. I still have some holes in my writing and I am always learning. I intend to use editing support for the rest of my life because ASL is my first language. Period.

Now I am the EIC for SportsMX's digital magazine, which will be released within a few weeks. My reputation for being in charge and being this organized has gone out. It's a very exciting time now.

Luczak: Maybe I'm mistaken in this regard, but you appear to be the longest-lasting editor of *SIGNews*. What were some of the challenges you've had to face as editor-in-chief (EIC)?

Dans-Willey: Yes, I am the longest-lasting EIC of this publication, and this is one of my favorite accomplishments, really. The toughest challenge I had to face as the EIC was retaining my readers. It took a lot of resources, energy, and miles to do just that. When the financial situation got worse, we had to stop traveling, stop marketing, and try to do it online; we did see a huge difference between back then and now.

Luczak: When you became EIC of *SIGNews*, what were some of the things you'd hoped to accomplish? Did those things happen? If not, why not?

Dans-Willey: I had hoped to be the EIC for 30 years. I had so many dreams for this newspaper. Everything I have done, I would not change. I had hoped for this newspaper to go digital. That was the only thing I felt I did not push hard for. It is all about resources. We did not have that.

Luczak: What sort of changes have you seen in the Deaf community in regards to print and online journalism since you started?

Dans-Willey: They have gone digital! Haha. They are going for videos more than text now. They don't really care what is being said on the videos; they would just watch and spread the word, even if the videos are not as factual as the interviews published in the paper. Interviews done on videos are not as tactful as in print. You see body language and facial expressions more when it's online. I'm not so sure if it's called journalism, but they do and it sure has changed!

Luczak: Any bit of advice to those wishing to enter the field of journalism while being part of the Deaf community?

Dans-Willey: Don't give up. Keep doing what you do, improve in areas that you know you are weak in. Criticize yourself before anyone criticizes you. If you know how to do just that, you'll be great.

FRANK GALLIMORE
Editor

Even though I'd interviewed Frank's Deaf sister Rosa Lee Timm a while back, I was quite thrilled to hear about their joint publishing venture, a brand-new online magazine called *Kiss-Fist* that celebrates the visual and creative artists within the signing community. (For those who don't know what "kiss-fist" means, it's a transliteration of the ASL sign for "love," as in things and experiences, but it is not the same sign for "love" for another person.)

Raymond Luczak: What do you normally tell people about yourself when a Deaf person meets you for the first time?

Frank Gallimore: I'm the only one in my immediate family who isn't Deaf. The Deaf community is small enough that many times I meet someone who's met my sister or mother, both of whom are somewhat well known. I was educated in English literature and creative writing at the University of Oregon and Johns Hopkins University. I've always been passionate about reading and writing, particularly about my experiences growing up in the Deaf community.

Luczak: How did you become interested in the literary arts?

Gallimore: I'd have to say my interest began with my father and brother. My father's a very literate guy, a fan of Hemingway, Kipling, Poe, and so on. He raised us to appreciate such things, and I'm thankful he did. As for my big brother Jed, I looked up to him quite a bit as a kid and wanted to emulate him. When he decided he wanted to be a writer, I did too. I started reading seriously when I saw him doing it. And it snowballed from there.

I received my MFA from Johns Hopkins a couple of years ago. There are pros and cons to every program, and none are created equal. While no one can teach you how to be a good writer, you can learn how not to be a bad writer, how to avoid common pitfalls and clichés young writers often blunder into. In that way, being given the time and attention to write and get constant feedback was very helpful.

Luczak: How does having a sister like Rosa Lee help you as a writer?

Gallimore: Rosa Lee's a great inspiration. Always has been. She's got the spirit and the guts to strive for the most captivating and serious artistic statement. I mean "serious" not in the sense that it lacks humor but that it is something to be taken seriously, that when you see her perform you know you are in the presence of someone truly in control of her message and craft. She knows what she wants and she perseveres. It challenges me to be more diligent and true to my own artistic vision.

Luczak: How did *Kiss-Fist* happen?

Gallimore: *Kiss-Fist* was Rosa's idea. We were chatting one day and she asked me what I thought of editing a magazine in which we get to showcase all the great work that's out there that perhaps hadn't had its chance yet to shine in public. Of course, I said yes. It's a family project and it reflects us, what we kiss-fist, particularly what we know of by word-of-hand, as we like to say.

Working on the magazine is tricky because we live on opposite sides of the country. Rosa Lee lives in Massachusetts, and I live in Washington State. We both review all our contributors' work via the Internet, and we discuss changes via email, IM, and videophone. There's lots of software involved, and luckily I don't deal with that aspect as much. My job is to look at the submissions and make sure they're appropriate and ready for publication in *Kiss-Fist*.

The success of the design of the magazine and its online interface is due to my sister's hard work, as well as her soon-to-be husband Damon Timm's superb technical know-how. She's done great work hunting down new contributors for the magazine, keeping our mag fresh and relevant.

We'd like to see *Kiss-Fist* on paper, so our readers can put their hands on it, subscribe to it, and perhaps pass a copy along to a friend. But we still enjoy the accessibility of the Internet, and how media-friendly it is in terms of vlogs, hyperlinking, and reader interaction.

Despite the unfortunate decline in newspaper and magazine sales, the boon of the Internet is that it has led to an even greater democratization of information. Anyone can check out our website and comment on what they see, and it doesn't cost a dime. Readers have more power and control over their reading experience; they can filter, react, participate, and contribute. Anyone online can go on whatever forum they choose, access, and alter the flow of discourse. The nature of public information has evolved into something that hasn't quite fleshed out its form yet. Technology will no longer constrain so much of it into a one-way medium as it has before.

LEAH ANGSTMAN
Writer and Editor

When a friend told me about Leah Angstman, an editor involved with the Alternating Current Press, I was immediately interested. However, she doesn't advertise her deafness, which intrigued me even more.

Raymond Luczak: Tell me a bit about your educational background.

Leah Angstman: The public education system, gosh bless it. Steele Street Elementary School, Mason Middle School, Mason High School, Lansing Community College, Michigan State University: the list goes on. My mother was an art and science teacher, so I started hard and started early, as a straight A student, freaking out at an A-, stressing over tests, and crying if a teacher was less than impressed with work I thought perfect, flawless handwriting, always the last one finished with a test. By first grade, I was tackling young adult books. In third, I did an oral book report on the themes of Salinger's *Catcher in the Rye*, and a shocked teacher called my mother to ask if she knew what I was reading. My mother's reply? Hamlet was always her favorite bedtime story. By high school, I was keeping a journal every day, taking every Creative Writing class for which I could qualify, Advanced World Lit, English Analysis, and all the boring bits, as well as being managing editor of the school newspaper and several years into the small press. On multiple full-ride college scholarships, I was a musical theater major, sick of school, active in everything, hopping from college to college, several published books under my belt, building my own theater, and roughing it alone just shy of the full-on degree. Just couldn't muster up that last math class.

Luczak: Would you mind talking about your hearing loss, and how's that affected your worldview?

Angstman: Ah, and now a question I don't get asked too often, as I am quite slow to mention my deafness. But yes, I suppose it is an issue. I was born with no conversational-level hearing, a fact my parents didn't know until I was well into talking-age. Teachers and family just thought I was an incredibly difficult child, quick to learn visually, but slow to understand verbal commands unless they were screamed at me. It wasn't until I was older, sitting on the couch with my mother, watching TV, when I said to her in my broken beginner's English, Mom, why are their lips moving, but they aren't saying anything? Her face went white. It took years to gain the knowledgeable ground that I should have had as a developing child, but as a visual learner, I was years ahead of my peers, which is where I credit my love affair with art, painting, colorful musicals, bright colors, theatrical opera, dancing, ballet. After 15 sets of tubes and several botched surgeries, I was left with holes and very little vibration capabilities in both of my ear drums and scars that my otologist called my "battlefield." The result was the restoration of most of my conversational-level hearing, but only temporarily, as it progressively gets worse each year. I'm not sure I can really say how it's affected my worldview, since I've never known what it's like to hear perfectly, so this is just all I know. What I have noticed is that people are far less patient of the deaf, even maybe afraid of communicating with them, often treating them as if they can't comprehend or process quickly, which will always baffle me, as deaf clearly does not equal slow. Through the small press, however, I can maintain some deafness-anonymity, as no one needs to know unless I choose to tell them, since I don't need or want it to be the focal point of any aspect of my artistic career. Through emails, letters, websites, and poetry, no one can know or judge me based on that fact, and it levels the playing field.

Luczak: What brought you to the literary arts?

Angstman: Initially, I would have to say my venture into the literary arts came from music. As a young'n, taking music and voice lessons and being enamored with story-telling songwriters, I wrote lyrics. Terrible, terrible lyrics that blossomed into the terrible songs of a 13-year-old kid. But in 1997, my best friend was killed in a car accident ten days before my 17th birthday, and that singular event spiraled me into a much different, deeper emotional mode: grief poetry. Shortly thereafter came my first chapbook, and thus a sorrowful loner was propelled into the world of the poet.

Luczak: What do you hope to accomplish with Alternating Current Press?

Angstman: When I began, it was called Propaganda Press at first. It started as an outlet for energy and grief, an outpouring of sentiments over the loss of my best friend, outrage and anger about politics, venting of a youthful rebellious underground society. I started the press because I have a big mouth and needed a place to yell. The first zines from Propaganda started around 1994, and the books are still going strong today. As for what I hope to accomplish with this, well, I think it's the same that any press hopes to achieve: to rocket myself to fame and roll in the riches! Ha. And live peacefully on my oceanfront property in Arizona. No, really, I think we're just here to accomplish dripping a splotch of needed art onto a sad world, onto anyone willing to listen and read and write and watch and buy and change his mind. We won't get rich, but if we just touch a few people, enrich a few lives, give a few opportunities, then we've left the world much better than we found it. Sound like a canned answer? Then let's just stick with getting rich!

ILYA KAMINSKY
Poet

When I came across Ilya Kaminsky's award-winning book of poems *Dancing in Odessa*, I was surprised never to have heard of him. After all, I was a Deaf poet myself and I thought I had met pretty much anyone in the Deaf community who wrote poetry!

Raymond Luczak: Tell us a bit about your beginnings in Russia and how you lost your hearing.

Ilya Kaminsky: When I was four years old, the Russian state doctor said I had a flu while I really had a bad case of mumps; so the nerves [in my ear] died. But in a Russian grade school, being deaf was often thought equal to being mentally unstable. Being both deaf and Jewish made things even more complicated. So I refused to wear hearing aids as a kid. I had the illusion that if I didn't talk to others, my deafness would disappear.

When I was 16 years old, my family received asylum from the American government and so, in early 1993 we arrived in Rochester, NY. There, I had no choice but to wear hearing aids for the first time in my life since my Russian lipreading skills were basically useless in American high schools. The attitudes to deafness in this country are vastly different: My classmates regarded my TTY as some sort of "magic boxes" that allowed me to "secretly" communicate with the teacher during the class—and I was more than happy to let them have that illusion! After high school, I got my B.A. at Georgetown University and then graduated from law school.

Luczak: How did your interest in poetry begin?

Kaminsky: Well, most teenagers write poetry—and most of them stop at age 16 or so. For whatever reason, I kept going. Perhaps because it became for me a way to understand my life and my time. One thing I can say for certain is that I didn't plan on writing poems in English. When my family left the Ukraine abruptly in 1993, I was still happily writing in Russian. Then my father died in 1994. But I couldn't write about his death in Russian—it'd hurt my family. And, above all, writing beautiful poems about his death in a language he taught me somehow seemed immoral. That I could not allow myself. But I had to write, and English was my refuge. I practically did not know the language, but I didn't care. Writing in a new language was for me a living embodiment of a poet's great line: "Death thou shall die." I like all sorts of poetry, from old Latin poets to ancient Chinese to contemporary Polish and American poets.

Luczak: In your book, you said that you became deaf at the age of four. Yet, in the poem "Joseph Brodsky," you described yourself as "hard of hearing." What's going on here?

Kaminsky: Well, here is what I want to tell people about my hearing loss but don't often get a chance: People often ask me what does it mean to be "deaf" or "hard of hearing," and the truth is—I don't know. Because I don't know what it means to fully hear. Does anyone fully hear? What is hearing? Now, the technicalities. For the purposes of "disability classification," I am considered "legally deaf." My audiogram labels my hearing loss as "profound." What do I tell people? I tell them to smile. Because I do not know what it means to be "hearing," my "deafness" for me is an imaginary condition.

Luczak: Do you ever use sign language? What have your experiences within the signing community been like?

Kaminsky: I studied ASL in high school. When I lived in Rochester, I was a lot more fluent in the language than I am now, unfortunately. My experiences with the signing community can only be described as: wonderful, wonderful, wonderful. There is a fantastic community in upstate New York that I was a part of, and I miss it sorely these days. But, recently, I have made new friends who are fluent in ASL and also in Russian Sign Language, which makes me happy. Sign language is a beautiful world; it is full of poetic motion and stillness. I think I learned quite a bit from it for my own writing, particularly in terms of image and humor.

LOUISE STERN
Writer and Artist

I was excited to learn about Louise Stern's short story collection debut *Chattering*, and the more I read up on her, the more I wanted to know about her. She is an American living in London, England.

Raymond Luczak: Could you please give us a quick overview of your background as a Deaf person?

Louise Stern: I am the fourth generation Deaf on my father's side, third on my mother's. I grew up going to the California School for the Deaf, Fremont, where my parents worked and where my brother and sister went to school. After that, I went to Gallaudet, like my brother and sister, parents, uncle and aunt.

Luczak: What made you realize that you were indeed into art? What kind of art did you make? Who were some of your role models?

Stern: Growing up I recognized something in books and art that I couldn't find anywhere else, and that I needed. I never thought of myself as an artist though, and it was only after I moved to London that I began to make art—first out of bits of the handwritten conversations that I used to communicate with hearing people. The painter Francis Bacon and the photographer Roger Ballen are among the artists whose work strikes deep for me, and I think of them when I think about what is possible through art.

Luczak: It sounds as if your work is similar to Joseph Grigely, who used scrap papers of written conversations with other people like wallpaper for his shows. Could you describe your processes involved in a bit more detail?

Stern: I use written conversations in sculptures and text works to look at broken narratives and their texture. I am interested in how language works in relation to emotion, space and time. I also use video and photography to look at the same.

Luczak: What about your interest in writing? How did that come about?

Stern: After I grew frustrated with the response of curators to my art, I thought writing might be a more direct way to say the things that I needed to say.

Luczak: Have you ever felt discriminated against or put down because you were a female artist/writer? Or do you feel that you've gotten more flak as a Deaf artist/writer?

Stern: What I am obsessed with is with language and how our society is increasingly addicted to defining via language. It's scary how far this addiction seems to reach. If you see art or writing as coming from a specific perspective straight off, then you will probably not see the work itself for what it is. Which is to say that yes, I have often felt pushed toward being seen as a woman artist or as a Deaf artist, but I don't want to engage with that any more than necessary. It is a waste of energy better used to make art or to write. All my answers that have any real meaning or real emotion are in my work.

Luczak: What prompted you to move to England?

Stern: A desire to get away from familiar surroundings, familiar ways of seeing and being seen.

Luczak: Aside from the obvious differences between ASL and British Sign Language (BSL), what were some of the notable differences between the American and British Deaf communities that struck you? And what about the non-signing communities in the UK toward you as a deaf writer/artist?

Stern: I felt that often non-signers here in the UK were less politically correct about deafness. I'm not sure if this is true, or why this is. The common language in this country often seems more concrete, and that might have something to do with it. As for the Deaf community, in Europe and especially in London, everyone can afford to travel. That means there is more chance for fresh energy and ideas to come in and out of the Deaf community.

Luczak: Do you feel that art is political? Or should it be more political? Or is it necessary for Deaf artists to be more political?

Stern: There are many sorts of art. I think the best, most universal art is not political in the sense that you mean. Certainly it hopes to illuminate the human condition and that leads to political truths rather than ephemeral political realities. It depends on what sort of art you hope to make.

ROBERT ARNOLD
Inventor of si5s

I met Bob Arnold a number of years ago when he ran the ASLian Poetry and Storytelling Night at the Bowery Poetry Club in New York. Since then he's gotten a B.A. in Deaf Studies from California State University – Northridge (CSUN) and a M.A. in Deaf Studies from Gallaudet. He now lives in Los Angeles, California where he teaches ASL. In the last few years he's been perfecting si5s, a new form of written ASL on paper.

Raymond Luczak: Weren't there written systems to depict ASL on paper developed before you came along? Do you know anything about the history of such systems?

Robert Arnold: When William Stokoe declared that ASL was a language he put in a notational written chart as an analysis tool to better understand ASL and its function. Stokoe made it clear that his chart of symbols were not meant for writing—that it was not a written system, just a tool. In the early nineteenth century Roch-Ambroise Bebian, a hearing man whose godfather was Abbé Sicard, felt a need for a written system of French sign language. He began this quest to establish the system and made good points as to why it was necessary. But he did not finish his quest as he shifted his focus to serious matters of employment at a Paris deaf school. He published his works as an essay. Sign Font came up in 1974 in San Diego. It was a computer-based model, not a handwritten one (although it can be handwritten). Valerie Sutton, a dancer who developed dance writing, came up with the Sutton SignWriting Notational System to note signing movements and non-manual signals of sign languages around the world. Notational writing is a form of making notes of something, that the information is specific. Music sheets, math formulas, and other forms of writing are notational writing. Written English, for example, is not notational where it tells the reader how to speak words but contains information for the reader to deduct the message.

Luczak: What prompted you to pursue the idea of si5s?

Arnold: In 1991 I sat in the chair, as each morning, starting to write a mystery novel. A question struck me: "If I cannot write in my own language, then who am I?" I realized that writing a novel was a double act of writing—interpreting my ASL thoughts into English and then writing down thoughts. I knew then that a written ASL system was needed, but was it possible? I did not pursue this right away. It was easier to write that novel in English, I thought.

What prompted me to start this were two books: *Wittgenstein's Poker* by David Edmonds and John Eidinow, and *The Professor and the Mad Man* by Simon Winchester. The former book discussed language philosophy and politics of two men, Karl Popper and Wilhelm Wittgenstein. That book made me think a lot about our existence as ASL users and how so much ASL had provided for our society has been largely unseen and only because there was nothing else to convey every facet of ASL but through sign language interpreters and videos with subtitles. The latter book discussed the establishment of the *Oxford English Dictionary* (*OED*). The tedious task of compiling that book took 70 something years, but it raised the standard of the English writing system, and it became a major corpus of the English vocabulary. For years we attempted to establish an ASL dictionary, but the problem was that it was not a written system. It was nearly impossible to create a reliable book of collected words to serve as an easy reference guide. Then and there I realize we had to have a written system so that we can then have a dictionary, like the *OED*, and that we can become transparent as society for so many to see—we no longer have to glide by like two ships in the night. The rest of the hearing world deserves to know all about us and our language, and it is an offering to them to acquire ASL.

Luczak: What gave you the courage and confidence to develop such a thing?

Arnold: As I mentioned earlier, the frustration of having the lack of identity in writing, the lack of ASL corpus and standardized ASL, and courses on writing at UCLA Extension back in 1990-1992 put the muscle into my task to develop si5s.

Luczak: What makes si5s different from these previous attempts at showing ASL on paper?

Arnold: First, si5s is not notational writing. Second, it is a handwritten model with the emphasis on the ease of writing each digibet (handshape) with five or less strokes. Other systems are computer- based or have too much strokes per handshape and other symbols that it became tedious to write. As a writer since 12 years old, I realize the importance of having the ease to write characters.

Luczak: Could you say that it is a written language, or is it still a system for showing ASL on the page?

Arnold: Yes, it is a written language. It does show ASL grammar structure and prosody in print. It is now easier to understand the ASL structure as a whole by glancing the page where you cannot while viewing a video in ASL.

Luczak: To someone who doesn't know how to read si5s, it looks very intimidating. Do you have to be a linguist in order to master si5s?

Arnold: Not any more than one should be a linguist in order to learn and master written English. In fact, my ASL 1 students had no difficulty in learning to write in ASL. I suspect it is because they have acquired a written system already—English, Spanish, etc. For this I came up with a theory of W1 and W2. I believe that in order for a deaf child to master written English—W2 (written second language), that child need to master his/her written ASL, as W1—written 1. This W1 – W2 formula is similar to the L1 – L2 language acquisition formula. If hearing ASL students have no problem learning written ASL ,why has it been that the deaf children have problems learning written English? I am convinced that once deaf children master written ASL, they own the language and they decide what's grammatically right, what's a clear writing style—the power to master a language among peers rather than having a submissive ("have to know") usage of a language like written English. Give a deaf child a language in written form, anywhere, at any time, in far flung places where there's little or no deaf population, and that child will grow in ASL, and would be in want to learn another written language because of the confidence in writing would be instilled in that child. This is my theory.

Luczak: What have you learned from others while developing si5s?

Arnold: It is a well-known fact that L1, first language acquisition, provides a solid foundation for second language learning, L2. Here, ASL students learn si5s with so much ease that shook me a bit until I realized they had a written discipline already, W1. That foundation made them eager to learn another written language without much of a fuss. However, for ASL users there has been a lot of fuss on learning written English. That would be the second language learning in written form. Where's the first language in written form if ASL is considered L1 in manual discourse?

Luczak: Could you tell me why you chose the name "si5s"? Couldn't you have come up with a more marketable or more memorable name?

Arnold: I wanted a name that truly reflects ASL in its own form, not translated into English. Deutsch is a German name for Germany and its language. But we use "German," not "Deutsch." I wanted a name for ASL writing in written form first. Si5s represents signing in ASL so I wrote si5s. In English, si5s best represents signing in ASL. The English word for si5s is ASL and written ASL. I want to retain the spirit of ASL as much as possible by using the term "si5s" for English, but in written form it's pure and represents exactly the prosody of signing in ASL.

Luczak: Do you think that si5s will enable ASL to be taken more seriously as a language in the creative arts, or do you think it'll become another niche development in the ongoing history of ASL?

Arnold: Both. It will show the seriousness of ASL as a language and unifier of deaf people in its society as well as outside of it. In a form of language ambassadorship, the written system will carve many niches in education, law, politics, linguistics, the arts, and more.

It will establish a corpus for interpreter training programs. Like what the

OED did for the British society, literature, law, science, academics and so on, in promoting and unifying the English language, this si5s corpus will enable the interpreters a vast collection of ASL spacabulary (spatial words) and provide better translation services. This also goes for transliteration. And how about this: There are millions of books, articles, and essays in English that are waiting to be transliterated into si5s. It is a vast industry waiting for the ASL community to capitalize upon and make a living from this. And there is a vast collection of literature in manual form, experiences, stories and more nestled in the minds of ASL users across the land waiting to see the light of day in print and transliterated into English and any other languages worldwide. For all time.

I cannot imagine our world without our written system. A new world to be created and written into this world in the hands of ASL users is happening now.

MARK DROLSBAUGH
Writer

Even though Mark Drolsbaugh and I have never met in person, I'd heard of his work as a Deaf writer. I thought I should email him some questions.

Raymond Luczak: For those who've never heard of you, can you tell them what you typically tell acquaintances for the first time?

Mark Drolsbaugh: For the first 30 seconds I say I'm a high school guidance counselor by day and a writer by night. Then I mention I'm the proud dad of three kids and spend the next 20 minutes bragging about them. :)

Luczak: What led you to writing? Who were some of your mentors?

Drolsbaugh: At the Germantown Friends School I had some really good writing teachers. Roy Farrar, Mally Cox-Chapman, Tom Scattergood, David Sanders, and Peter Reinke had a major impact. They taught writing, yes, but beyond that they always encouraged students to find their own voice. In fact, there were some things I wrote that were really way out in left field, but they encouraged it because I was expressing myself. Ultimately I learned that the two secret ingredients to being a good writer are originality and passion. Find your own style and believe in what you say.

Luczak: Much to my embarrassment, I've never read your book *Deaf Again*. Can you tell me about it? Does it fit in with our national debate over Deafhood?

Drolsbaugh: *Deaf Again* is an autobiographical account of how I survived in the mainstream—did quite well, actually—yet something was missing. That something was the Deaf community and as soon as I enrolled at Gallaudet University, it was like everything came together. It's the classic mainstream vs. Deaf argument, and I was on both sides of the fence. A lot of people mention "oral failures" but *Deaf Again* points out that it's possible to be an oral success and still miss out on a lot of good things in life. So the frame of reference is what makes this book unique. What makes the book odd is the fact that the whole time this was going on, I grew up with deaf parents. Hearing relatives and medical professionals ordered them not to sign with me and to keep me in the mainstream at all costs. I had to find the Deaf world myself even though it was right there under my nose. As for Deafhood, this book could be Exhibit A. It chronicles my progression as a hearing toddler, a hard of hearing child, a deaf adolescent, and finally a culturally Deaf adult.

Luczak: Do you have Deaf children? How is it different for you?

Drolsbaugh: Whew, I could write a whole 'nother book about this. Yes, my oldest son Darren (aged 11) is Deaf. I do feel he has an advantage because his parents have been through the same thing (my wife, Melanie, is also Deaf). Not only does he have more language access, but it also means a lot to him when we "get it" as he deals with some of life's inevitable frustrations. Another advantage he has is a wide range of Deaf role models. He's met Deaf adults from all walks of life including teachers, lawyers, medical professionals, entrepreneurs, athletes, and entertainers. As a result he knows that the ability to hear is not a prerequisite for success. It's all about the mind and belief in yourself. A few teachers at school were concerned because Darren prefers not to wear hearing aids (he finds them uncomfortable). He's not worried at all because his grades are good. That's the important thing, and we're fine with it. At the same time, going back to the Deafhood theme, this is his journey and not ours. What I've learned is that instead of just teaching him about the deaf and hearing communities, it's best to let him have full access to both—and let him find his place in the world on his own terms. It's a wonderful growing experience for all of us.

Luczak: What are your plans in the future? Any exciting projects?

Drolsbaugh: I'm working on a spinoff of *Deaf Again*. It's tentatively titled *Drolz Uncensored: Madness in the Mainstream*. It's going to feature stories that were too raunchy or too politically incorrect for *Deaf Again*. Some of these stories were left out of *Deaf Again* because I wanted to keep it clean—I knew that Deaf kids with similar experiences would read the book. But now that I'm the parent of a Deaf kid, it's time to write a book that takes a closer look at what really happens in the mainstream, even when you succeed in it. Right now a lot of deaf programs are being cut, and more emphasis is placed on mainstreaming. There are so many Deaf kids who miss out on opportunities to interact with Deaf peers and role models. *Madness in the Mainstream* will be a wake-up call for parents and school districts, and I'm hoping it'll help halt the trend of cutting programs for deaf and hard of hearing children.

My web site, Deaf Culture Online, discusses many of these issues. It's all about awareness. There are many things about being Deaf that the world still needs to know. If people are able to understand our perspective, things are more apt to change for the better. That's the motivating force behind Deaf Culture Online.

JOHN LEE CLARK
Publisher and Editor

When I learned that the Tactile Mind Press (TTM) was going to close down *The Tactile Mind Quarterly*, I was quite disappointed. Sure, I was one of their writers, but I really admired my publisher's vision for his company. Quite a few folks asked me what was going on with TTM, so I decided to ask John directly.

Raymond Luczak: Why did you set up the Tactile Mind Press? What were some of the challenges?

John Lee Clark: When I was a student at Gallaudet, I met several talented writers who, like me, were trying to find ways to share work with our community. But I found that there were no real outlets for us. So I decided to establish TTM. I wanted people to be aware of our community in more intimate ways, as opposed to just in the academic sphere. This intimate awareness is for both those inside and those outside. And I believe that our books and DVDs have done a great deal here.

One of the first things I learned after beginning work on our first magazine issue in late 2000 was how differently Deaf writers treated their own work than those in the mainstream did. In the mainstream, every single literary publication has mountains of submissions. They just flood in from writers all over. This didn't happen to us, so my job description resembled that of a bloodhound more than a regular editor. I had to hunt down writers. Many were shocked that their writings were worthy of publication, so I had to do some handholding. And there's always this problem of finding someone who evidently writes, coaxing that person into showing me work, only to find that it is not good enough for publication. But I love challenges and I seem to have a natural gift for working with all sorts of people and under all sorts of circumstances.

Luczak: Do you feel that the signing community has been supportive of TTM? Why, or why not?

Clark: This is a complicated question. First, we do have support. But not always enough. For example, we had to close down the magazine recently because we didn't have enough subscribers. We did a subscription drive, but we failed to meet our goal even with new subscriptions. As with many aspects of Deaf life, it is hard to tell whether it is a Deaf-related problem or a problem true of any community. Take the mainstream: Most literary publications operate at a loss, so they are almost always affiliated with institutions such as universities. There is not enough support in the mainstream to support literary publications. But we were the only literary magazine for our community on an international level. Some of our foreign subscribers have expressed their surprise that the relatively large signing community in the United States could not support the magazine. And there's a whole other dimension to the issue, that of cultural values. Written English, after all, is not indigenous to Deaf culture. But I don't know how important this factor is, given that we do produce DVDs of ASL literature that only a few Deaf people have bought. The DVDs are doing well, thanks mainly to interpreters and hearing people interested in ASL. We could probably do much better by catering to them, but we are determined to promote authentic stuff.

Luczak: What are you most proud of as the publisher of TTM?

Clark: My greatest reward has been the knowledge that it has, through the powerful writings that we have published, saved some people's lives. We've had readers writing to us to say how a story, a poem, or an article has changed their perspective and helped them to love more who they are as Deaf people. This is one reason we cannot stop what we are doing. Maybe literature is not important to most people, but it is absolutely necessary to a few, and that is good enough for me.

MICHELE WESTFALL
Writer

I've known Michele ever since our college days at Gallaudet, and of course, I'd been reading her work in print since then. I thought it'd be fun to catch up with an old friend.

Raymond Luczak: When you meet a Deaf person for the first time, what do you normally tell her about your educational and family background?

Michele Westfall: Other than my name, the Deaf person gets to learn that I'm a Maryland native, grew up in Deaf schools in MD/DC and graduated from MSSD. The Deaf person also learns that my family is all hearing and my mother used SEE while I was growing up. My father, brother and sister all use manual alphabet to communicate with me. Not ideal, but certainly better than being oral.

Luczak: How did that affect your interest in reading and writing while growing up? Did you have role models?

Westfall: I come from a family of readers, so I was always exposed to books. Writing is another matter entirely, as nobody in my family or at the Deaf school did that. I had no role models for writing, unless you count authors of various books I've read.

Luczak: How did you become involved with the writing business? I seem to recall seeing your work for the first time in *Deaf Life*.

Westfall: I started subscribing to *Deaf Life* approximately a year after they started, and they had a regular feature called "Faxview Poll" where readers voted and commented on a question posed by *Deaf Life*. The publisher Matthew Moore liked my comments and thought I should start writing for *Deaf Life*. I resisted at first because I didn't think I had enough material in me to sustain a regular column. After a year (or so) of persistent prodding by Matthew, I changed my mind and agreed to write "Beyond the Envelope." But in actuality, this wasn't the first time I got involved in the writing business, only the first time my writing became known to the Deaf public! The first time I got involved with the writing business was when I was at MSSD and a dorm counselor asked me to proofread his draft. His draft got published as a book titled *Reasonable Doubt* and that was my first official credit and entry in the writing business.

Luczak: Do you think your writing has evolved since *Deaf Life*? If so, how? Where do you see your writing headed?

Westfall: Writing is an activity where one gets better with practice, so certainly my writing has gotten better over the years. I've written for NAD and other companies. I have edited several books. Currently I'm a freelance writer and I do some writing and editing for ASL Rose, a Deaf-owned company. I also have been working on and off on a book about the history of Miss Deaf America pageant since 2000. Life keeps interrupting that particular project, but eventually I hope to finish that book and work on my next historical and/or biographical book.

Luczak: What are the challenges of doing a biographical/historical book about the Miss Deaf America pageant? What drew you to that project? What does it mean to you personally?

Westfall: When doing a biographical/historical book such as Miss Deaf America pageant, I have found that hearing media is a poor source, since they tend to focus on the "lack of hearing" aspect of the deaf person and ignore almost everything else that is remotely interesting about the deaf person. It doesn't mean that they don't occasionally print some concrete information that I can use in my book, though! Deaf print media, on the other hand, has been an invaluable resource for this type of book. The big drawback is that Gallaudet Library and Archives is the only major source of Deaf periodicals, and most of them are not indexed. I spent hundreds of hours physically going through every Deaf periodical on their shelves reading through page after page to get nuggets of information. It was hard work, but I believe ultimately worth it. I used to work at NAD as their Youth Programs coordinator, and the pageant was one of my responsibilities. I was also responsible for coordinating Miss Deaf America's travel schedule. So I have seen firsthand how much the program benefits Deaf women, and the pageant has always been a popular draw at every NAD conference. Society has always been into looks and always will be. It's human nature. What I have always liked about the Miss Deaf America pageant is the fact that it has never had a swimsuit category, and that it has no weight limit. Overweight Deaf women have competed in the past and some of them have done well (the last one I remember ending in the top ten was Miss Deaf Oregon in 1994). Hearing pageants cannot compare to us in that regard, and I think it is something that many Deaf people forget. It's easy to complain about pageants being about "looks," but one cannot discount its obvious benefits for Deaf women. No other program provides Deaf women this much training and exposure to people, leadership, and performing that Miss Deaf America pageant does. Additionally, we all need a touch of glamour, and the pageant most definitely provides that for the Deaf community. Most importantly, NAD isn't "shutting it down" . . . it is merely adding "ambassador" to the title and allowing Deaf men to compete. This ultimately changes nothing. I'm fine with that.

Luczak: Have people ever accused you of being too Deaf-centric? What would you say if that was the case?

Westfall: Culturally Deaf people have never accused me of being too Deaf-centric. They always have been fans of my work. I typically hear it only from oralists, dysconscious audists, and/or their hearing supporters, and I regard that as par for the course. (A dysconscious audist is a Deaf person who internalizes negative attitudes held by the hearing society, to the point where s/he is unable or unwilling to appreciate the positive things about Deaf culture, signed languages, and Deaf people.) They're certainly never going to approve of any Deaf person who practices values and beliefs of Deaf culture and most especially those who actively advocate for ASL and Deaf culture. I don't just write, I write to advocate. I have two Deaf children, and I am passionate about the future of Deaf community, and this is how I contribute to the well-being of Deaf world. I'm also very keenly aware that there aren't that many culturally Deaf writers out there who consistently put out pro-ASL and pro-Deaf culture work, and I believe this is sorely needed. You know how a ripple moves through water? It starts out small at first and eventually makes a big wave before hitting the beach. This is how I see the eventual impact of culturally Deaf writers . . . it will take some time, but eventually we'll take the beach.

BLINK OF A LENS

ARTHUR LUHN
Filmmaker

A few years ago someone sent me the link to the Boston-based Deaf filmmaker Arthur Luhn's web site, which contained a few video clips of his work. I became more interested when he was promoting the DVD version of his feature film *The Golden Legacy*.

Raymond Luczak: What led you specifically to make films? Did you just pick up a video camera and go, "Gee, I'll do this now"?

Arthur Luhn: No, I didn't pick up a video camera; I stole it.

Luczak: You stole it? How?!?

Luhn: I'm afraid that must remain a murky matter. I used a credit card without any thought of paying it off. This is common among guerilla filmmaking, but I want to strongly discourage this, as things have a way of getting back to one. It's not a practice I want to encourage because your credit rating takes a bad hit, but on the other hand, a true guerilla filmmaker never listens to anyone. The word "no" is not in his or her dictionary.

Luczak: So tell me something about your first short film.

Luhn: Making *Destination Eyeth* was a lot of fun. Naturally I used my carpentry skills to slap together all that fancy gizmos and gadgetry you see. Plus I have a great love of the silent films by Charlie Chaplin, Buster Keaton, and Fatty Arbuckle, and that first film was more or less a homage.

Luczak: What about your second short *Earadicators*?

Luhn: It was about a family finding a foreign substance on their property, which turns out to be a hearing aid. I just covered some subjects that I wanted to explore. *Earadicators* isn't really elaborate; it was just a simple story unlike *ASL Trials*, my third short.

In *ASL Trials*, there are four individuals who are obviously incompetent, and they're trying to pass the standardized requirements for becoming an authentic ASLian, an user of American Sign Language. They go through several tests. With this I was trying to convey that one had to get past being in awe of and being intimidated by an authority that is more or less medical-based, which says that you may not assert yourself in any other way than being disabled, and then the next escaping being implanted. The final test is a riddle that I leave to the viewer.

Luczak: Let's move on to *ASL, Inc.* What inspired it?

Luhn: The key event in *ASL, Inc.* was the conflict the main character was experiencing. He needed to have his needs supplied, but then he'd have to accommodate the definition that society has given him. The character attends a meeting during which money is allocated to each party; he is obviously soliciting for funds, but while there, he has to endure being lumped together with people of varying differences, and being labeled "disabled."

So what does he do? Does he boycott and just walk out without having his needs supplied or does he just keep his mouth shut, just take his punches and walk out with the dough? But during the film, he daydreams in which he finds a third way. He walks out of that meeting as a symbol of rejection, rejecting the label that's on him, and dreams of being able to build something, a new identity, a new corporation that he builds, ASL Inc. As in a daydream, everything happens easily, and he gets what he wants. But he wakes up and realizes that it was a dream; he finds himself back where he was—do I take the dough and the disability label, or reject both?

Luczak: What prompted you to make *The Golden Legacy*?

Luhn: Two words—Indiana Jones. I just love that franchise. Actually there is one other reason. I was just so sick and tired of watching movies made about Deaf people from a hearing perspective, and seeing that stigma of loneliness and sadness and self-pity, so repeatedly associated with deafness. *The Golden Legacy* is a light, upbeat movie. It's fast and full of action. Not heavy and slow and full of meaning—something like an antidote to the poison that's out there in terms of portraying Deaf people.

Luczak: I saw the original silent version of the film on videotape. Is the DVD version going to be any different?

Luhn: Yes. The silent version is 112 minutes; the sound version is 94 minutes. We have a fabulous original score by Chris Thoft Brown, and quite a number of great songs by artists such as Jimmy Dorr and Dan Krentzman who are recognized artists on their own. This version was cut by a very accomplished and talented editor, Noah Lydiard, who also served as producer, so the bells and whistles are out on this one!

Luczak: *The Golden Legacy* used community actors. Was that a conscious choice, or was it a lack of enough professional deaf actors in the Boston area?

Luhn: I'd love to say it was a conscious choice, but the truth is that was a clever piece of guerilla filmmaking. Most people would not see this, but I was greatly frustrated with what I could accomplish with that film. My creativity was greatly limited by the lack of resources, lack of money, which meant a lot of creative aspects had to be left out.

Luczak: Any word of advice to Deaf people who want to become filmmakers?

Luhn: One of the biggest problems that Deaf filmmakers face is putting aside their personal differences in order to work in a professional capacity. Most Deaf people do not see that the person most talented is not always the most likeable person, but if you want to have a solid product, you just have to put aside personal differences. The other big piece of advice I have is to get a network going—not just develop a network but take care of it as well. Left on its own, networking/network will die out, so you must maintain consistent exchange, including thanking people. These are basically social skills that go a long way. The thing here is that social skills in the Deaf culture are different than that of the larger world; you get away with more, but this doesn't really work in the world at large.

Luczak: Do you feel that Deaf people don't look at things positively or tend to criticize too easily?

Luhn: It is my experience that in Deaf culture, criticism is unabashed. Faults tend to be zeroed on. I have received a lot of criticism in regard to *The Golden Legacy*. Most of them were pointless, and that's another bit of advice for Deaf filmmakers. They have to ignore the criticism and believe in their visions, not to let the criticism bog them down or discourage them in any way.

ORKID SASSOUNI
Photographer

When I learned that Orkid Sassouni, a deaf Iranian woman I'd met at various events over the years, had become the new president of Deaf Performing and Visual Artists (DVPA), a Deaf arts-related organization in San Francisco's Bay Area, I had to ask her about her career as photographer.

Raymond Luczak: Please tell us a bit about your background.

Orkid Sassouni: I was born in Tehran, Iran, and I became deaf at around age three due to a fever combined with ear infections. My family moved to America, and I grew up learning to use speech therapy on Long Island. A doctor had told them that if I used sign language, I would never speak. Even though I am in constant touch with them, they still haven't accepted my deafness even today.

I had wanted to go there so badly when "the world heard Gallaudet" in March 1988, and I was so shocked that there was a college for Deaf people! So I knew I had to go there even though my parents objected to the idea. I had grown up in a public school where I didn't have support of any kind. I had to sit in front of the classes to speechread my teachers. I learned ASL at Gallaudet.

Luczak: Have you had any shows of your photographs done?

Orkid Sassouni: I've done solo shows and group shows. I started out during my college years at Gallaudet University as a major in Art History and Museum Studies. I decided to submit a picture for the school's Annual Photography Contest. So when the judges announced the winners for the third, second, and first places, I was literally not paying attention to the announcements. I was talking to a friend until everyone started to stare at me for a while. I was like, Is something wrong here? My teacher told me to walk up to the stage. As I walked onto the stage, I still had no idea what I'd done wrong until I guessed I'd won first place for my one photograph. Ever since that day I bought a new camera and became hooked to working in the darkroom.

I started out taking photographs of my family and gaining experience that way, but when I took photography at Gallaudet, I took six rolls of black-and-white film, and guess what? All the images came out blank. I was about to give up on my interest in photography until my instructor was laughing. I was like, What's so funny about it? She said that is a very good mistake. I was like,

Huh? After learning my mistakes, I realized she was right. Photography training requires a lot of mistakes until you reach perfection. You cannot be perfect the first time around.

Luczak: So what did you do wrong with those six rolls of B&W film?

Sassouni: I didn't roll it enough when I started shooting. You know how you put film in the camera and how you have to manually roll first to get it started? If you want to become a serious photographer, don't start with automatic cameras. Those snapshot cameras are for consumers, and with the manual cameras, you can change the light situation, angle, perspective, and so on.

After my contest win, I bought a new and light plastic camera, a Vivater. My old camera had been really heavy in my hands. The quality and approach changed with this new camera, and it was then I realized that antique cameras could still take very good pictures. It was all about the quality of the lens that enabled me to capture the right light. In the word "photography," "photo" means "light, and "graphy" means "to study." That's what photography is about a study of light. Meaning, with my camera, I was looking for a light that really affected the mood of the images itself.

With my Vivater camera, I felt more like a tourist, taking pictures all over the place.

I decided to change over to a Nikon camera that was both automatic and manual. I still wasn't happy with it, so I decided to enter the Parsons School of Design to study photography a year after I graduated from Gallaudet.

I discovered my strength as a photographer in the 4-by-5 camera, like the Sinar. That camera gave me a lot of freedom to play with light, as if I'm a magician. Even though the Sinar is hard to work with, I had more freedom to play with light, pushing for more depth and twisting the images.

Luczak: How long were you at Parsons?

Sassouni: I went there for two and a half years. It was the most intense schooling I've ever had. My instructors were always critiquing my work, especially with my projects that focused on being Deaf and being free-spirited. One of them was not happy with the size of the images. I never wanted to make huge images of the Deaf community in my project, and so the subject matter and the technique bothered him. Of course, the technique could've used more improvement, but he didn't really understand why I focused on the Deaf community.

At first I annoyed my Deaf friends with my constant flash as it really affected their communication in between, so I decided to experiment without flash. The images weren't good so I pushed even further until I nailed the right formula, developing the ASA 400 film as if it's ASA 1600 film. The results were amazing, especially when they were printed small with a Polaroid quality. They were more like documentary pictures.

I still love that darkroom thing. I love the magic that comes out on paper.

SHANE P. DUNDAS
Television Producer

Long before I learned that a deaf producer had nabbed the "Producer of the Year" Award from the Broadcast Professionals of Wichita, I'd known about Shane's relentless drive. But I wanted to know more about him.

Raymond Luczak: What was your childhood education like?

Shane P. Dundas: I was born profoundly Deaf, with a bilateral loss of over 120 dB. I started wearing hearing aids at the age of ten months. I was put into an oral school first in Wichita at the Institute of Logopedics (now Heartspring). Then I moved to Oklahoma City, where I continued to have oral training until I went to Vanston Middle School in Mesquite, Texas. When I was 14 years old, I learned ASL. I later went to Samuell High School in Dallas. Prior to my move to Texas, I had attended oral programs in Oregon and California.

Luczak: Why all that moving around?

Dundas: I'm a third-generation broadcaster. My dad was in the radio, so we moved as the markets got bigger: Wichita, Kansas; Oklahoma City; Portland, Oregon; Santa Cruz, California, then to Texas. Dad was an on-air personality, which is the same thing as a DJ; he played oldies and rock 'n roll.

Luczak: How did he feel about you being deaf, given his job?

Dundas: He has been very supportive; he always helped me learn how to speak, read lips, etc. He even encouraged me to learn ASL if I needed to. Mom is extremely supportive, but she was very strict during my years in oral schools; no ASL was allowed in the house, but during high school, she was fine with it.

Despite the ill perception of oralism, I had wonderful teachers in wonderful schools. I was never abused or anything like that. My oral teachers instilled in me the pride of being a Deaf person. I also had great support from my family and relatives as well as friends, both from school and the neighborhood. So, now, I have the very best of both worlds, being both Oral Deaf and ASL Deaf.

Luczak: How did you prepare for your career in television?

Dundas: First I went to Friends University in Wichita for one semester and majored in Social Work, but it was really an undecided major. I quit school for two years because I didn't know what I wanted to do with my life. I wanted to be an artist, a deacon, a travel tour guide, a foreign language interpreter—many things. I was pretty flaky at the time. But I met a reporter/anchor for the ABC affiliate here in Wichita, who became a very good friend of mine. She gave me a tour of the TV station, and I instantly fell in love with television.

When I met her, I had to go back to college, this time to Butler County Community College. Then I transferred to Wichita State University (WSU). I majored in Broadcast Journalism there and graduated with honors in May 1997. I was also awarded as an "Outstanding Broadcast Student of the Year."

Luczak: How did live reporting work for you? Any goofs?

Dundas: I did quite well with the speech therapy at WSU preparing me for live reports. It was challenging because it was such a conscious effort to speak correctly. It changed my life because it made me a brave person.

Yet when I came on, I became more confident. I knew where I stood. When the red lights came on, I just did it, and then when the show ended, I'd take a huge breath and be so relieved. According to others, I had a great on-air presentation (facial expression, body language, etc.), but of course, I do have an "accent." The speaking part was my biggest challenge.

But I had no goofs. In fact, at the end of the year, a reporter wanted to do a special on bloopers made by all the student reporters and anchors, and this guy, who is a friend of mine, tried hard to look for the goofs I'd made. I hadn't made any!

I had learned all kinds of things—film work, editing, filing in the traffic department. I did everything I could get my hands in. I had to look at various TV stations all over the country for a job. In fact, most jobs I looked for were in the range of 100 to 140 market size, which is small.

But I couldn't really find a job in the broadcast industry after graduation even though I had won a few national awards from the Community Broadcasting Association. Everyone wanted to work in television, so the competition was fierce.

After four or five years, I was just "this close" to giving up on my dream and do whatever it took to get any job to survive, even though I volunteered my time and energy at a local community TV station just to keep up my skills. I was ready to apply for a factory job in Wichita.

Then I got an email from Kansas' Warner Brothers (it was called WB33 at the time), asking to meet with me. I ended up going back for two more interviews. I had to "sell" myself to them and convince them that they wouldn't regret hiring me as I would have the least liability to the company because of my hearing disability.

Luczak: What did you do as Producer in those first days?

Dundas: The pressure was on me from the station, so I had to work harder to prove myself to the folks, in the same way that many minorities do. The first three months I constantly worked around the clock, making sure that everything was running smoothly. I learned quite a bit during the first year, and I'm still learning. I wasn't being taken very seriously. It was so difficult even though I gave input and ideas, which they shot down. But my situation changed for the better late last summer.

I started taking notes of my suggestions, and then when they failed with producing a local show, they were like, "We should've done this and that." I'd show them my notes, which proved that I had proposed such ideas to them. I think they're starting to take me more seriously now.

Some people would blame me for their mistakes. Like, "The spot is due at 4 p.m.," and no one told me anything, so they'd blame it on me because they failed to tell me. I may be deaf, but I ain't dumb.

I told my boss one day, "Either you trust me or you don't. If you don't, I'm outta here." I guess he's learned to trust me since then.

Luczak: Do you have a funny story to share with us?

Dundas: One time, between interviews I've had, I clipped the wireless microphone on me as my hands would be full, and then I left it on when I went to the bathroom. When I came out, people were laughing at me. I was like, "What's so funny?" Boy, was I embarrassed! But soon, I was laughing too.

BILL CRESWELL
Online Captioner

Because I was working on a play about Helen Keller, a friend alerted me to an online clip of Ms. Keller herself. I was surprised to find it subtitled, so I emailed the hearing man who's apparently on a mission to provide subtitles for movie trailers and whatnot. The tag line for his web site reads "Captioning the Internet one video at a time. So many web sites, so little to say (so I caption what others say)."

Raymond Luczak: What were your growing up years like?

Bill Creswell: I grew up in Michigan, born to great parents, both very smart and well spoken. I was the youngest of five, and therefore was essentially an "only child" after age eight. I spent most of my days riding bike all over town, playing with my best friend, collecting Matchbox/Hot Wheels cars. I was quiet in school, and "never performed to my full capacity" (space cadet—that's me). I sang solos in church and was in choir most of my life.

Luczak: When did you first become aware of deaf people?

Creswell: Having grown up in this town, I probably wouldn't have easily recognized the difference between someone with hearing loss, and someone who was deaf. Helen Keller, Marlee Matlin, *Mr. Holland's Opus*—that would be about all I knew. In fact, a guy I used to talk to at the gym spoke and read lips so well, I had no idea he was deaf. I tend to mumble, and he understood me as well or better than most. I became aware of his deafness later.

My first experience with a known deaf person was a Showtime complaint online. After following her blog, and the rest of DeafRead, I can't say much has changed about my impressions of D/deaf people; they're still people. I have learned more about the Deaf culture, deaf experience. I have currently served more than a year on the board of Deaf and Hard of Hearing Services in Grand Rapids.

Luczak: What were your initial thoughts about closed-captioning (CC)?

Creswell: I've always liked CC—I use it at the gym, since earphones don't stay in my ears when I run, and when I walk, I usually read. I like to see the captions when there's a news story or something on. I also use CC at night, when my wife is trying to sleep, so I don't have to turn it up to understand. TV volume varies a lot, especially TV ads that often have louder sound levels than TV shows. Some of my children like to watch with CC on, especially movies. Sometimes you don't realize how much dialogue you don't catch.

Luczak: How did you become aware of the fact that so many videos online weren't captioned?

Creswell: It started with the Showtime complaint. I started thinking about captions, and even went to a movie using the reflector. It bugged me that the trailers weren't captioned. I looked around and couldn't find a captioned trailer for the movie we were playing, so I made one, and linked it to the movie. After I posted a couple on my own blog, DeafRead started to publish some of them, and my views jumped from four a month to more than 150 a day; the last two days has seen 3,500 views!

Luczak: How do you determine which videos to caption/subtitle online?

Creswell: I try to do all the trailers from the MoPix list first, then requests, and then ones that I find interesting. I generally use Overstream.net. Overstream allows you to select a video from several online sources, add captions and fuss with the timing, and even export your captions. The Overstream player plays the original video from the sources, with a layer on top with the captions. That's not the technical description; I don't know the details, but because Overstream doesn't host the videos, it prevents them from worrying about the video copyright issues. That's left to MySpace/YouTube/DailyMotion to sort out, since they store the clips.

Without a transcript, the way I normally have to caption; it takes me about 45 minutes to do a three-minute video. I can cut that to 20 minutes for a music video that has lyrics available online. I don't charge. I did try Google ads, but it generated $12 over a year. Plus it just doesn't work as well as my normal VodPod video collection site, which makes collecting, tagging and searching easy. The WordPress site is free, so I can't do ads.

It's cool though, just giving back. Wordpress is free, YouTube/MySpace is free, Vodpod is free, Overstream is free. I can do a lot with free tools, and I give back free. It's like a game, keeping up with the caption movies each week, adding videos, adding views. It's also a lot more valuable than the time I could easily waste on video games, spider solitaire, or dicewars.

As far as full time work, I don't know. There are people who are trained to do this stuff—professional transcribers and captioners. I don't want try to compare my amateur work to the stuff that they do. I'm still learning. But in the short term, I like what's happened. I have made friends online (just got a "you rock" from Shoshannah Stern for the captions on her latest movie trailer). Three web sites have made regular use of my trailers, adding them into their site.

I do wish that movie companies would just do the captions themselves. Such a small investment—an hour of captioning, by people with a transcript—hey, they could even have an intern do it. It's not that tough; it takes just a little time and commitment.

JULES DAMERON
Filmmaker

A lovely perk of doing these interviews is that I'm able to get to know exciting artists with drive, passion, and goals. Jules Dameron, a Deaf filmmaker, was no exception.

Raymond Luczak: What were your educational experiences like growing up? How did your family feel about your deafness? Do they sign?

Jules Dameron: I've been deaf my entire life. I always attended school mainstream-wise. I'm from Minneapolis, Minnesota, and attended a really great high school program. There were at least 40 Deaf and hard of hearing students at the time I was there, in a school of 1,400. There were a total of seven working interpreters and six teachers that taught classes only in ASL. This high school had a great arts and media department, so there was a lot to learn there. In short, I think I led a fairly optimistic life growing up, heavily had a passion for filmmaking from the very beginning, or at least started when I was seven. My parents and family weren't Deaf, so they, of course, found a challenge in raising me. But they were always positive, supportive, and encouraged me to do whatever I wanted, no matter what it was. My mom signs, and my father semi-signs. But the point is, really, that they were completely communicative with me, at least one on one. However, whenever the entire family was together, it'd be tough for either one of my parents to interpret everything, and they always felt obligated to do it. There was some issue in that, but then again, we all did the best with what we knew.

Luczak: Tell us a bit about your filmgoing experiences.

Dameron: The first film off the top of my head is *Moulin Rouge*. I've always been kinda obsessed with that film, in terms of visual expression, story, characters, music, everything about it. It is visually inventive, and I love that. Aside from that, I was always obsessed with the television series *Star Trek: The Next Generation*. I just absolutely adored the concept of it, and the stories it told. I never get tired of watching any one episode.

Luczak: Did you go to college? What did you study?

Dameron: I went to Gallaudet University and majored in Television Cinema for my bachelor's degree. I felt that I needed an experience to solidify who I am, as a Deaf person since my schooling experiences involved ASL, and I liked the 100% communication using ASL, but I felt that there was a tremendous wealth of information I had to learn from being at Gallaudet. So because of that experience, I'm basically a complete person in how I view myself today.

My second college was the University of Southern California (USC). I got a Master of Fine Arts degree in Film Production. After learning about myself as an individual, I felt like there was one area of information that I had not enough access to, and that was filmmaking. I knew that filmmaking is an incredibly complex process, so I wanted to go someplace that would make me become an excellent filmmaker, and learn the filmmaking system that had already been developed. In addition to that, I got to do everything in school that was completely hands-on. It was much more action than lectures, and that, above all, was the best and key element of going to USC. I actually feel much calmer knowing what to expect when coming into creating a film and knowing what I want, and how to make it happen. Before USC, I had much fear about creating a network of people that I didn't know, and probably didn't use ASL to communicate. But now, I completely feel that this was the best experience of my life.

Luczak: What led you to the world of filmmaking?

Dameron: I was seven, like I mentioned earlier. I attended a family reunion one day. My uncle was holding a handheld VHS camcorder that was attached to the television, so you could see whatever he was shooting simultaneously. That got the rocks in my head moving. "So . . . that's how it's done. The magic behind the screen? That's it. It's a camcorder." Once I discovered that, that gave me the biggest disease of all: passion to create something that impacted people.

Luczak: What do you hope to accomplish with your work as a filmmaker?

Dameron: I want to be able to achieve two things—one's a short-term goal, and the other is long-term. The first goal is to achieve quality work in acting, characters, and story. Those things, above all, matter the most when making a film. I also want to be able to achieve the best work possible with Deaf actors and using ASL without feeling like you can't connect to them. The long-term goal is that I essentially want to be able to financially support myself doing what I love to do: directing films. Right now, I'm in the red, but that's usual for most starting companies and filmmakers.

RONALD DANS
Board President, D-PAN

When a friend alerted me about the Deaf Performing Artists Network (D-PAN), I was intrigued by its focus on involving Deaf people in the music industry. Ronald Dans, its board president, agreed to talk with me.

Raymond Luczak: What's your educational background?

Ronald Dans: I grew up in Ontario, attending Milton School for the Deaf which is just outside Toronto, until I was 11. Then I went to the Robarts School for the Deaf in London, Ontario. I graduated from there and went to work for a while, but I soon decided that I had to do better, so I eventually graduated with a degree in Business Administration from Gallaudet. I am the Department Head of the Interpreter Training Program at the Oakland Community College in Michigan; I now have 16 years of experience in the education field.

Luczak: What were your feelings about music while growing up?

Dans: Music to me was never audible, but I could always enjoy the rhythm, the bass and the vibrations. Music was also enjoyable to me when made visual, especially at concerts. I could watch the drummer, see the costumes and outfits, watch the light show and the singer's body language—all of those things are music to me. The vocal part never really interested me, but because I am Deaf, seeing the visual effects and feeling the rhythm together was always very enjoyable, and I knew other Deaf people could enjoy it too. My best friend, who is hearing, took me to huge headliner concerts in Detroit. I was a little uncomfortable at first, but I grew to love it when I could sit and watch hearing people out of their seats, dancing wilding and moving their heads back and forth. It made the music more interesting.

When I was very young, my father took my hand and put it on his old wooden radio. He knew I had wondered why he would look at it, and that was my first exposure to music. I could feel its vibrations and experiment with it, turning the volume up high. Eventually I would sit and watch TV with my arm on the radio, watching TV and feeling the radio at the same time! I also remember that my hearing siblings loved their music. I tried to read the lyrics whenever I could find them, but I never really understood until my sister explained that lyrics were just a story about whatever the singer was singing about. He was opening up his heart and talking about his experiences the same way we all do, but he was just using music. Now I love feeling the vibrations from many different types of music.

Every time my family went to a wedding, it was the same old thing—hearing people out dancing, enjoying the music and Deaf people (my Deaf brother and his Deaf children) sitting around, talking. I was not the type of person to sit and be left out. So I asked one of my sisters to sign the words while we danced. I loved the dancing, but of course I couldn't hear the music. Eventually we moved near the booming speakers, and then it all started to come together.

Luczak: How did D-PAN come about?

Dans: I had a conversation with Sean Forbes, a Deaf man who can hear enough to enjoy music, and sign and sign with it. He asked me if I liked music. I told him I loved music, especially the bass. Shortly after that he introduced me to Joel Martin, who owns a music studio. I also met Scott Guy, who had over 15 years in the music industry. It was awkward with different cultures and languages, but we all wanted to find a way to give Deaf and Hard of Hearing people the same access to the music industry that hearing people have. I know that most hearing artists come from a different place than Deaf people do; but we are not trying to force two cultures to become one but to have two worlds share each other's art and culture.

Luczak: What's the response been so far?

Dans: After we set up D-PAN a year ago, we shot our first music video. We brought in a Deaf woman, Rosie Switras, and Sean, and got a really great response. Before that there was no music videos made for Deaf and Hard of Hearing people. It was amazing to get feedback from many different people. A lot of it was positive, and some of it was negative, but in those negative comments, we got a lot of inspiration and direction. Our intent is not to force both cultures into one mold, but to bridge the gap while respecting differences in cultures and languages. I remember from the time I was young, knowing how important it is to respect ASL—maintain it, develop it, and nurture it. It's also important to be known that we as Deaf people should always try to open doors and know that we can do anything we want. D-PAN is a great opportunity to share our language with the world. That's what we hope to accomplish while we're waiting for the world to change.

LOUIS NEETHLING
Filmmaker

Earlier this year when I was in London, I couldn't believe my luck when a friend who worked on *Switch*, the popular Deaf soap opera running on BBC, invited me to watch a scene being directed by Louis Neethling. It was so fascinating to observe how he, a Deaf man, dealt with directing not only the actors but also the framing of the shots through the use of remote cameras in a van. He was busy then, and he is busier now that the editing of the new season of *Switch* is being completed. Still, he was gracious enough to answer some of my emailed questions.

Raymond Luczak: How did you become deaf, and how were you educated?

Louis Neethling: My family is Deaf. I went to St. Vincent's School for the Deaf in South Africa. All of my family went to the same school.

Luczak: What sign languages did you learn? Was it different between the ones used in South Africa and Great Britain?

Neethling: My native sign language is South African Sign Language (SASL). My mum is British who has influenced me with her use of British Sign Language (BSL). She grew up here in England and had emigrated to South Africa after the Second World War. I think BSL is more formal than SASL. Luckily, there isn't such a big difference between SASL and BSL.

Luczak: What were your first impressions of film?

Neethling: When I was a little boy watching *Star Wars*, it was a magical place to be.

Luczak: What were your conceptions of being a filmmaker like before you actually took the plunge into shooting?

Neethling: Well, I was a presenter first of all and I always used to watch the TV director by following him about when I wasn't in the shot. I wanted to be able to do the same thing but as a Deaf person taking control of the Deaf TV program. I quickly realized that the power, creativity, and satisfaction came from being the director of the program/film. I thought it would be easier to get projects moving otherwise.

Luczak: What were some of the films/TV programs that inspired you?

Neethling: Frank Darabont brilliantly directs the film *The Shawshank Redemption*; he keeps you glued to the screen until the very end. The style is simple, but everything is in the details. TV in South Africa was not subtitled so it was only until I moved to the UK that I appreciated how good some of the stuff on TV is!

Luczak: What led you to your work on *Switch*?

Neethling: I moved from South Africa to the UK to work for the BBC. *See Hear* decided to start a Deaf soap (*Young and Speechless*), and I had experience in that area. *Switch* was launched in 2001 to celebrate the 20th anniversary of *See Hear*. Before this, Deaf people had rarely featured in television drama but *Switch* brought them center stage, dealing with the issues that affected them. The response to *Switch* has been overwhelming. The show was discussed in Deaf clubs and pubs; used as an educational tool in Deaf schools and sign language classes—but overall simply enjoyed as a television drama operating in the "soap" genre. Its appeal has now spread far beyond the confines of the Deaf community to the extent that the cutting edge *Face* magazine named it as one of the top 20 programs on British television in 2003! Jana Bennett, the BBC's Director of Television, described *Switch* as "an innovative project which really connected with its audience. It was a groundbreaking drama which had something to say about the lives and experience of Deaf people and its basic themes appealed to all sections of the audience."

Luczak: Has your initial views of *Switch* changed from the first episode to now? What's different about the new season?

Neethling: Yes, it has changed. The development and growth of the Deaf actors' skills in TV has had a big influence and of course, the budget! It's a fact that if your budget improves, your facilities for making a classy production improve! The storyline has also improved with each series.

PERRINE DAILEY
Digital Artist

When a friend of mine suggested that I look at the deaf artist Perrine Dailey's online portfolio, I was most fascinated.

Raymond Luczak: What drew you to art?

Perrine Dailey: Being an artist came to me naturally. Perhaps it was a gift I inherited from my artistic maternal grandma, or maybe art didn't require me to hear or speak. I use art as a source of personal healing which allows me to reach inside my soul and pull out hidden ideas and emotions.

As an adult, I began to experiment with computer-generated art, including fractals, which are mathematically generated swirls of color. I printed my fractals on holographic paper for an intriguing 3-D effect and mounted and framed each piece. These fractals were extremely popular and I have had several shows featuring my fractal art.

Luczak: What was your training like?

Dailey: Being mostly self-taught, I pride myself on being able to figure out how to best use art tools and supplies to make something new and unusual. Most of the time I enjoy the process of learning about art through trial and error. I did have formal art training at Augsburg College [in Minneapolis, Minnesota] where I studied art history and sculpture while earning a degree in Sociology. My clay and plaster creations were nothing to brag about, but I did create some beautiful alabaster stone sculptures which later won awards in juried shows. I loved the feeling of using a hammer and chisel to slowly remove rock to expose the sweeping lines of an abstract creation that lay hidden underneath.

A few years ago I enrolled in a series of Community Education classes taught by a local sculptor named Helene Oppenheimer. The classes were called "ASL in Clay," and the participants created handshapes and ASL letters with clay. The class was interpreted and the students were a mix of hearing, hearing-impaired, and Deaf people all working together. I was greatly inspired by Helene's De'VIA and her dedication to sharing a new art form with the world.

Luczak: What were your experiences with the signing community like?

Dailey: When I lost the majority of my hearing at age three due to an infection caused by croup, my parents decided I would wear hearing aids, speak, and be mainstreamed. I did not know other deaf people until I reached high school, and even then, I felt like they were different from me. But because of my inability to hear my teachers despite my hearing aids, my grades suffered. Thanks to an intervention from a wonderful deaf social worker, I began to use an interpreter and note-taker in my classes and began to excel. I also began to make a few deaf friends, which helped ease the sense of isolation I had felt. I took classes to learn ASL, but even to this day, I don't consider myself fluent. My younger sister is also deaf in one ear and had learned some sign language too so we can sign to each other.

In college, I wanted to take an ASL class to fulfill the "foreign language" requirement, but the school refused to accept it as an alternative. I petitioned the school, with help from the staff at the Center for Learning and Adaptive Student Services (CLASS Program), where I worked as a student secretary for three years, and much to my relief, my petition was accepted. I took two intense ASL classes at the University of Minnesota that summer and it was the best immersion in ASL I could have hoped for. My battle with the school over their "foreign language" department rules resulted in the school changing the name of the department to "modern languages" and they now accept ASL as an option for all students. I was awarded the prestigious Keymaker Award from Augsburg College and CLASS for my efforts to change the policy and "open locked doors for students with disabilities by finding a key."

Luczak: What would you recommend that budding artists do to further their craft?

Dailey: They should allow themselves to create and not hold back their emotions or ideas. Art is not necessarily shared with others. If the artist is brave enough to share their creations with others, then they may find that their works enhance the lives of those who see it. There is no bad art; just art that might not appeal to everyone. Creating art is a source of healing for the artist, a way of connecting with our own essence and making something that has meaning only to the creator.

DAVID H. PIERCE
Film Festival Producer

Even though David H. Pierce, a Texas-based Deaf filmmaker, and I have corresponded via email over the years, we've never met in person. Then I learned he was going to mount a film showcase of sorts.

Raymond Luczak: Where did you come from?

David H. Pierce: I'm a native New Yorker who attended public schools in the Buffalo area. After graduating from NTID, I relocated to Hollywood, California and then to Texas where I've resided for the last 16 years.

Luczak: What was watching movies like for you when growing up?

Pierce: I didn't have access to TV or theatrical captioning during the sixties and seventies, so I resorted to motion picture film collecting at age five with a focus on silent films with intertitles and films converted with subtitles to be played on projectors without sound. This "accessibility," which was intended for hearing people, was of obvious benefit to me. I didn't get a caption decoder until the mid-eighties, so I was mostly a "film" person most of my life.

Luczak: What led to your making movies?

Pierce: Since I started collecting films at age five, I naturally learned to "edit" them when I had to repair them or combine several films on a single reel to create programs. I started shooting at age eight when I bought an 8mm movie camera at a garage sale. I went on to video as a teenager and gradually went professional when I decided to make my avocation into my vocation. I've been working in the industry for 21 years now. I established Davideo Productions in 1986 with a partner, David Strom who now works for Sprint, in Rochester, New York. One of our clients was Silent Network, a national cable television network targeting deaf audiences, so I decided to close Davideo and move to California to work for the network. I worked there for 13 years until it shut down in 2000 when it was known as Kaleidoscope. (Silent Network eventually became Kaleidoscope in the mid-nineties). After Kaleidoscope shut down, I relaunched Davideo Productions as a Texas company. We are primarily a services-based business—providing production, post-production, and consulting services to clients including filmmakers, television producers, corporations, government agencies, and consumers. We're now in our sixth year of operation.

Luczak: What are you most proud of in terms of your work as filmmaker?

Pierce: My broadcasting career highlight was running a national cable television network airing in 15 million households 24 hours a day, seven days a week. It was 100% accessible with every show, commercial, infomercial, promo, and PSA captioned at a time when there were no FCC captioning regulations in place. I'm now working behind the scenes to get our new broadcast television programming service on the air—Sign City Television. I've reunited with former Silent Network folks to pull this off, including its founder, Sheldon I. Altfeld who started the network in 1979. We've already won a couple awards so far.

Luczak: What's Cinema for Everyone about?

Pierce: This is our third film showcase so far. The last two were successful and well attended with between 225 to 400 people. I use the word "showcase" rather than "festival" because we are a regular theatrical exhibitor with various film showcases throughout the year. We also have a cafe and bar involved to provide places for socialization while visiting Seguin, Texas. These showcases are a good venue for filmmakers to show their material to the general public beyond the "festival" circuit and making money from box office sales.

Luczak: Any word of advice for those who want to set up their own Deaf and/or accessible film festivals?

Pierce: Better incentives need to be provided to the participating filmmaker beyond just "exposure." A share of ticket sales would be more lucrative than forcing the filmmaker to pay a submission fee and not getting any money in return for exhibiting their work. The business model I've created for our film showcases accomplishes this goal when the filmmaker gets a share of box office ticket sales. The time for freebies is over. I know how it feels because I've had some of my own films shown at festivals, and I didn't get anything in return financially. It has to be a business, not charity. We need to eat and offset the costs of our productions.

MICHAEL PIMENTAL
Sports Photographer

I first became aware of Michael Pimentel's amazing work as a Deaf photographer when he shot pictures of my actors to promote a play at the California School of the Deaf, Fremont well over two years ago.

Raymond Luczak: How did you get into photography?

Michael Pimentel: When I was 12, I got my first camera, a Pentax. I shot on film ever since until about a year before I turned pro. I switched to digital with my first-ever digital camera, a Canon D30 with 3.1 megapixels. I built up my portfolio much faster with the new camera than with film cameras due to the cost of film development and prints. After turning pro, I used the D30 for a few weeks, and then went out and got the Canon 1D for the first two years. These days I use Mark IIs. I still use my old 1D cameras as remote cameras behind goal nets and backboard hoops.

I have always loved photography. In the beginning I focused on wildlife and breaking news events and showed off my work to friends. They weren't impressed because I asked them to be honest with me. I decided to try shooting sports so I got permission from someone at Chabot College to shoot games from the field rather than from the stands. I showed off my new sports photographs, and they were all shocked. They encouraged me to focus on sports so I shot more games to build up my portfolio in sports photography. I approached a few magazines with my work, and a few days later one photo editor at Fightnews magazine contacted me with a paying assignment to shoot the World Championship boxing at the Palace Gaming in Lemoore, which was shown on HBO. After that event, I got a few text messages from friends who had seen me on HBO. Over the years since then, friends have seen me on TV lasting from five to 30 seconds while shooting celebrations and coin tosses. I'm used to that now but I always make sure that I shave and trim my goatee so I can look good on TV.

Luczak: How did you get involved with the 2004 Olympics Games in Athens, Greece?

Pimentel: I had been shooting major league soccer and the Women's World Cup 2003 for two years for International Sports Images (ISI), an official photographer provider for US Soccer, for two years. The president of ISI was impressed by my work in soccer photography so he picked me out of 11 photographers from his company to become a team photographer for the US Women's Soccer team at the 2004 Olympics. I shot them in action when they won a gold medal against Brazil.

What's interesting is what happened when the United States Olympics Committee (USOC) learned of my deafness while trying to contact me over the phone for information like my Social Security number, passport number, and so on. They turned out to be very committed to the Americans with Disabilities Act (ADA) because they also run the Paralympics, so they were very aware.

Luczak: What's next for you?

Pimentel: My goal is to have a photograph of mine appear on the cover of *Sports Illustrated*. It would be a huge crowning achievement for my sports photography career. The magazine selects only one great photograph from hundreds of photographers around the world, and the cover is seen by millions of readers. Yes, *Sports Illustrated* has published about 60 of my pictures, but I've yet to make it on the cover. I'm working on that!

STEVE SANDY

Associate Documentary Producer

Over the years I'd been aware of Dummy Hoy, the legendary Deaf player who was so influential in the early days of baseball. It is criminal that his accomplishments haven't been given his recognition at the Baseball Hall of Fame. I decided to ask about this situation with Steve Sandy, the associate producer of the documentary *Dummy Hoy: A Deaf Hero*.

Raymond Luczak: Tell us a bit about your background as a Deaf person.

Steve Sandy: Moi—ASL? Of course I am an "ASLer." I was born in the Army but raised in the Air Force (my mother divorced an Army man, who was my father, and remarried an Air Force man), so we moved a lot around the country, including Hawaii, Pennsylvania, New Mexico, Washington, D.C., Texas, Pennsylvania, Alaska, Alabama, and Ohio. We even went to Spain. I have a hearing sister and brother. My wife is Deaf, and we have two hearing daughters aged six and eight.

Luczak: Did you play baseball while you were growing up?

Sandy: Yes, I did play in the right field with a hearing league before I went to the Model Secondary School for the Deaf (MSSD). I had some struggles as communication was the primary problem, but I was able to play with the support of my parents. Then I played baseball for MSSD but didn't get to play much since they didn't trust my judgment. I became the equipment manager, and then I left the team to get involved with drama.

Luczak: When did you first hear about Dummy Hoy?

Sandy: I never knew about Dummy Hoy when I was growing up. I was born and then one month later he passed away. Dummy Hoy died in Cincinnati, and I was in Honolulu, Hawaii. I began learning about Hoy in 1989 when I was involved with a Deaf organization in Toledo. I learned that they did propose to have Dummy Hoy in the National Baseball Hall of Fame back in 1987 but the motion was not active. They planned to remove their submission so I asked if I could take action on it. I asked just out of the blue. That weekend I was also elected as a state-wide president of that Deaf organization.

I began doing research on him. I got to know more about him than anyone else. There had been a number of Deaf people who had tried to get him into the

National Baseball Hall of Fame before I was born, but they failed. I found some old NAD articles where a group of supporters tried back in 1950 and 1951. But there weren't just enough votes by the Committee at the National Baseball Hall of Fame. But I did locate who the voters were. Connie Mack headed the committee but he was probably outvoted. There was another attempt in 1970, but that effort fizzled when it reached the higher levels at the National Baseball Hall of Fame. Keep in mind that Connie Mack and Dummy Hoy were teammates!

Luczak: Aside from the fact that he was Deaf, why should we care about Dummy Hoy?

Sandy: If it wasn't for Dummy Hoy, the barrier would still stand against Deaf people who wanted to play baseball. No one would be using hand signals on the field. They'd be using their voices, which would be so confusing. Through my research, I discovered the timeline in which it was impossible for the umpire Bill Klem to have invented baseball hand signals in 1905. This "fact" is stated on the wall at the National Baseball Hall of Fame. Dummy Hoy had retired in 1903.

Luczak: How did you get involved with the film *Dummy Hoy*?

Sandy: Through my research, I have gotten in touch with Dummy Hoy's family. I remain very grateful for their patience while supplying me with information that no library had on hand. Eventually Dummy Hoy's grandson spoke with a producer and director, David Risotto, and suggested that he contact me. From there, we emailed each other and we felt a strong connection. Within one year and one month at Louisville, Kentucky, we made an announcement in September 2007 to start showing and selling the film *Dummy Hoy: A Deaf Hero*. That felt fitting because Hoy had played for the Louisville Colonels in 1898. We eventually showed the film at the National Baseball Hall of Fame Festival.

During the process of making the film, David Risotto promoted me to Associate Producer. I was aboard as a consultant and responsible for a lot of the research required for the film. He stated that he couldn't have made that documentary without me. I felt so honored. Yes, David is hearing, but he has way too much respect for Hoy that he wouldn't change a thing without consulting me first, especially when it came to Deaf issues.

I was the one who suggested that Deanne Bray play Hoy's wife after I had a "screen test" with her. I was sitting a chair away from her while we talked about her work on *F.B.Eye*. A week after Louisville, I flew out to Long Beach, California where I met Ryan Lane, the actor who played Dummy Hoy in the documentary. He told me how he felt about kissing Deanne Bray was an awkward reaction. Ryan had not reached his 20s and feeling much uncomfortable in kissing a lady much older than he was. But Deanne Bray had taught him the ropes of how to be an actor. Ryan hadn't realized that Deanne's husband was playing the role of Dummy Taylor in the documentary. It was a chuckle to see Ryan realizing that her husband was there.

Luczak: Why is it so hard to get Dummy Hoy into the Baseball Hall of Fame?

Sandy: The committee is made of other people and former baseball players who then screen and vote on the ballot. It's very tough to get on the ballot. Education to the screening committee is the key. My source at the National Baseball Hall of Fame explained that it must reach 75% of the voting to elect a player or so into the National Baseball Hall of Fame. Apparently Hoy hasn't gotten at least 75% of the votes.

How can we change that? We need to get every person to write letters to the Screening Committee. If you write by hand or use an electric typewriter, please use the letterhead for your organization. That will count. You can also write an email to the Screening Committee, which they will also count. It's also important to sign a petition for Dummy Hoy's induction into the National Baseball Hall of Fame. Someone should coordinate such an effort, reaching out to Deaf clubs and other places, and then mailing it to the Screening Committee.

I asked my source at the National Baseball Hall of Fame about the number of signatures. Aw, come'n, only 25 to 50 a year? We need more than that! 100,000 would be a nice round number! Buck O'Neil, who was inducted recently in the Hall of Fame, had around 15,000-25,000 signatures.

Is that all? Uh-huh! Every Deaf person who knows something about Dummy Hoy should get in touch with their favorite columnists and reporters and get articles written up in newspapers and the media. They are welcome to get in touch with me for further info on Dummy Hoy. I will be happy to answer questions. As President Abraham Lincoln said, "a ballot is stronger than a bullet." So we need to educate more. I have given presentations on Dummy Hoy around the country.

KELLIE MARTIN
Photographer

When I asked my friend Lilah Katcher if she knew of other artists who might be interested in being interviewed, Kellie was one of the names that came up. After checking out her work online, I was naturally curious.

Raymond Luczak: Can you share something about your background as a Deaf person?

Kellie Martin: I recently graduated from Gallaudet University with two majors: Theatre Arts (Production) and Studio Arts. Before going to Gallaudet, I completed my high school studies at the Kentucky School for the Deaf. I also took a few courses at a local public school. I come from a hearing family with the perks of a few Deaf members in my family. Deafness is genetic in my family, and the deaf gene skipped a few generations. I have a young Deaf brother and a few Deaf cousins. Often, people would assume I come from a Deaf family.

My parents did not find out that I was Deaf until I was two and half years old. My parents did suspect my deafness; they did not have the right resources till late, which was common in the 1990s. The first thing they did, though, was to take ASL courses to communicate with me. In the early 1990s, my doctor recommended to my parents that I get cochlear implants. My parents were strongly against the idea. Six months before I was born, my grandfather had died from a brain tumor, and my parents lost trust in the medical system.

They strongly encouraged me to choose my own path and develop my own identity as a Deaf person. I am blessed, and so grateful, to have them as my parents because there are not many parents like them.

Luczak: When did you become interested in photography?

Martin: I've always liked photography but I never thought I had it in me, until I met Professor Michelle McAuliffe. Originally, I had to take a Digital Camera course under Professor McAuliffe for my Studio Arts major. To be honest, I did not want to take the course because I thought it would be a waste of my time. Uh-oh, I couldn't be more wrong! It changed my life.

Professor McAuliffe asked us what kind of photographs fascinated us. I had an epiphany: I remembered how my attention was drawn to black and white nude images. I always saw them as raw and beautiful artwork.

Luczak: Here in America, there seems to be an unfortunate bit of puritanism over the naked human body. How do you work with your models? Where do you find them?

Martin: I lost my interest and the ability to express myself in art because of the puritanical environment in Kentucky. That changed when I enrolled in Gallaudet. Its liberal culture helped me to find my artistic side again. I felt very overwhelmed, but I was excited at the same time. I never have felt so free until I discovered the beautiful form in nudes.

I had my own struggles with weight and body acceptance because of stretch marks. That made me feel insecure with my body until someone told me once: "Why do you work so hard on your body? What if you are still unhappy about it after you succeed? It's time for you to start and find art in your body. You are the artist of your own body." That's when I started to realize my own power. I wanted to change others' self-esteem and acceptance of their own skin by having them pose in the nude. I've seen how the media can destroy a person's self-esteem. It was and still is a challenge to work with models from the Deaf community, especially at Gallaudet. I wanted to have more Deaf models because I wanted to overcome the taboo of body acceptance within the Deaf community. I also wanted to make sure nothing awkward would happen, or something could harm the models before, during, and after the project. That's how I came up with the idea of doing the project without showing models' faces.

People contacted me via Facebook when I announced that I was seeking volunteers for my class project. A lot of people volunteered, and it was one of the best experiences I've ever had. I learned how to be patient and interact with people by setting up boundaries because the nature of the photo shoot was very sensitive. Whenever the shoot ended, the model and I would sit down and show the pictures. Their reactions amazed me, and they would leave with more confidence and acceptance. Through this process, I saw the depth of their souls.

Luczak: What other subjects continue to fascinate you?

Martin: I've recently started to experiment with portraiture for theater. The surrealist effects possible in Photoshop always has been a fascination of mine. My next project will focus on abandoned places in America and Europe.

Luczak: How would you summarize your approach as a photographer?

Martin: Being raw is the best thing because it's truthful. I want people to leave with a positive view of nudity from my work. The imperfections of people's bodies are meant to be celebrated in spite of societal norms in which "gender" is expected to behave.

MISSY KEAST
DVD Producer

When I worked with the actress Deanne Bray on the TV show *Law & Order: Criminal Intent*, she was quite excited about the imminent release of the DVD series *Your Pregnancy: What to Expect*, which she had worked on with Missy Keast. I had to learn more about Missy herself.

Raymond Luczak: Missy, what's your background as a Deaf person?

Missy Keast: Because my older sister was Deaf, my parents already knew sign language before I was born so they already had a good foundation of communication at home. I was so fortunate to have had a good education not only at schools but through my family. Colorado School for the Deaf and the Blind (CSDB) and Arizona School for the Deaf and Blind (ASDB) taught me well. I went to Gallaudet from 1984 to 1988, then I transferred to Arizona State University where I graduated with BA in History in 1993.

Luczak: You seem to be very much into teaching signs to babies. Is there a tangible benefit to having babies learn ASL?

Keast: There is a huge benefit to having babies learn sign language for early pre-verbal communication. Signing is so much easier than trying to voice using vocal cords, lungs, mouth, tongue, lips, cheeks, etc. Babies are able to express their feelings and needs in sign language. Of course any deaf mother already knows this. It is the hearing world that is slowly awakening to this fact.

Luczak: Didn't you and Deanne get pregnant around the same time?

Keast: Actually we took turns being pregnant. First I had Sage, now three years old. Then Deanne got pregnant, and six months later I got pregnant again. When we filmed in Sedona, Deanne was just a few days away from giving birth. Her daughter, Kyra, now is 18 months old and my second daughter, Spring, is one year old. It was wonderful having that overlap. She witnessed my first pregnancy experience and vice versa. We shared so much information and wisdom of pregnancy!

Luczak: What prompted you to make the DVD about pregnancy for Deaf women?

Keast: When I found out I was pregnant with Sage at my age, 38. I was so happy. I was so ready for it. But I realized that I had no idea what to expect during my pregnancy. I collected many books to read and got great information from my doctor. She was fantastic. But on an emotional level, I needed a mutual understanding of experiencing the pregnancy with women, and I could not find that. In the waiting room of my OB/GYN, other pregnant women chatted back and forth while I sat by myself wondering what they shared. While I was healthy and very happy, I had no way of really knowing what other women were going through. I realized that there were no ASL DVDs describing a pregnancy. Then Deanne became pregnant, and she was glowing. We talked a lot about what I had gone through and what she was going through. We also tried to sort through all the materials available for pregnant women, especially for pregnant Deaf women. There was not much. At this point we decided to do something about it. Her TV schedule had a nice break, and I already had a production company in place to produce ASL educational materials. This led to the three-DVD concept segmented by trimester. Our husbands were really supportive.

The project has grown a lot since that beginning. The best section—interviews with other pregnant Deaf women—was not even something we thought about at the beginning. Deanne started to travel again and interviewed more than 20 pregnant Deaf women around the country. She met many wonderful pregnant mommies along the way. She interviewed midwives, an ultrasound technician, mothers of twins, dads, and so on. One time she and Troy were grocery shopping, and they happened to meet a pregnant Deaf woman who is now in one of the DVDs. I have never seen another Deaf pregnant woman in the grocery store! Our three-DVD series will be a great resource for pregnant Deaf women, women who are thinking about getting pregnant, interpreters, healthcare providers, high schools and educators.

JOE CLARK

Accessibility Activist

When I first saw the web site captioningsucks.com, I was immediately intrigued. Joe Clark, who's responsible for the content on that web site, has been something of a gadfly for better captioning.

Raymond Luczak: Tell us a little bit about your educational background. Where did you grow up?

Joe Clark: I have a B.A. in linguistics from University of Toronto and a diploma in engineering from Dalhousie University, Halifax. I was born on Prince Edward Island and grew up in New Brunswick—not that it matters after living away from there for 30 years (the last 20 in Toronto).

Luczak: Have deaf people changed when you entered the captioning field?

Clark: I got interested in captioning when I stumbled upon *The Captioned ABC News* around 1978. One thing led to another.

The change among Deaf people has been generational: Older people who were subjected to the residential school system had rather poor literacy, but kids who grew up in mainstream schools (or just Deaf schools where everyone signs) had access to captioning, TTYs, and the written word in general. Young deaf people's literacy is hugely improved—you see that especially online now, with the many deaf blogs.

I do find that the older generation thinks captioning should behave the way it did in 1980—heavily edited, badly positioned, SHOUTING IN CAPITAL LETTERS. (They think it still does behave that way.) Younger people want near-verbatim captions (partly because they can usually keep up with them), and they are much more sensitive to lousy captioning.

Luczak: What does closed-captioning mean to you? Why do you care even if you're hearing?

Clark: If hearing people didn't care about captioning, there would be no captioning.

I've been interested in captioning for so long (since I was about 13) that I just cannot remember a time when I wasn't interested. So I have a hard time explaining what it means or why I care. At this point, it's simply built in.

Now, captioning got me interested in accessibility for people with disabilities, a field I've worked in most of my adult life (and the subject of my first book *Building Accessible Websites*). Captioning is one of the fields of accessibility that interest me. But it isn't the most important one, or the least important, because deaf people aren't more or less important than anyone else. The whole point of accessibility is equality, so I can't go around playing favorites.

Luczak: What are some of the things that need to be changed in the captioning industry?

Clark: Well, standards, of course—that's why I'm trying to get my research project, the Open and Closed Project, off the ground. There are no independently-developed, researched, and tested standards for captioning (or audio description for the blind, or subtitling or dubbing). We want to change that. Much of the time, when you see lousy captioning, it's because the captioner didn't know what they were doing, or thought they did but were wrong.

The other thing that captioning viewers should worry about is the race to the bottom. You've seen this yourself—cheap scrollup captioning on shows that shouldn't use it (you should never see scrollup on a fictional program), or real-time captioning on shows that aren't really live. Broadcasters can barely restrain themselves from acting like cheap bastards when it comes to captioning. They didn't get in this business to help cripples, and they think captioning gets between them and their profits. Well, it does get in the way, but broadcasters (and video producers and so on) have an ethical obligation, and often a legal obligation, to provide captioning.

But at the moment, so many broadcasters are so filled with resentment at having to caption at all that they shop on price. That's why you get postproduction houses—the same places that duplicate broadcasters' tapes—pretending they know how to caption. Or non-native speakers of English, like Filipinos and Indians, pretending they know enough to caption U.S. or Canadian (or British) English.

As a captioning viewer, you have very little recourse when you're stuck with lousy captioning, because it's next to impossible to file a complaint (isn't the show already over?), and anyway, you shouldn't have to complain: You have a right to a service equal in dignity (or quality) to the service hearing people receive. That's why we need standards, and those standards can't be written by industry, because they don't know what they're doing, and their entire focus is shaving a fiftieth of a penny off the price of an hour of captioning.

Luczak: What do you hope to accomplish with your new web site captioningsucks.com?

Clark: To shock people out of their complacency. I want people to quit pretending that having a lot of captioning on a lot of shows means we don't have any problems. There's still too much uncaptioned video out there; captioning, in general, is awful, because broadcasters are cheap and captioners are untrained. Captioning really does suck. Now let's fix it.

RYAN COMMERSON
Activist Filmmaker

Even though some people may've had issues with Ryan Commerson's activism, I still found his online film *Media, Power & Ideology: Re-Presenting D-E-A-F* to be very provocative. Sometimes the best kind of activism happens when one is confronted with things one must think about instead of putting them off for another rainy day.

Raymond Luczak: Didn't you go to Gallaudet? If so, how did Gallaudet help you as a Deaf person?

Ryan Commerson: Yep, for both my B.A. and M.A. degrees. Gallaudet helped me realize that the worst form of audism can be found at Gallaudet. I didn't like what Gallaudet was, but I love what Gallaudet could become. Its very institution has been steeped in paternalism and ironically, that alone helped make me a stronger person with a clear vision of what needed to be done to remedy the entrenched problems that's enveloped Deaf people.

Luczak: You studied film at a college in Michigan. What did you learn from that process?

Commerson: I attended the Motion Picture Institute of Michigan, a certificate program. I learned that hearing people wouldn't give Deaf people a chance because it's not their place to do so; it's up to Deaf people to carve a spot in the film industry on their own.

Luczak: I seem to recall that you led a grassroots effort to help improve the Michigan School for the Deaf. What was that like?

Commerson: It was an intense experience. It took two years of emotional turmoil before a protest took place. I learned that Deaf people's fear of losing the school was so strong that they would turn against their own people (me) for trying to make it better. Upon the recommendation to read *Rules for Radicals* by Saul Alinsky, I was finally able to set aside my emotions and think rationally, looking at the situation as a game, playing tactically, and it worked. I want to emphasize that I did not act alone; a friend, Alison L. Aubrecht, was an equal game changer. Without her, none of this would have ever happened.

Luczak: Do you feel that there aren't enough Deaf activists? If so, why aren't there more? What could be done to help remedy that situation?

Commerson: Indeed. There can never be enough activists in general because the job's so inconvenient. Who would foot the bill? First of all, Deaf people have long been cheated out of language and education from the minute they were born. There must be an ideological shift in order for this problem to be remedied; hence, the film, *Media, Power & Ideology: Re-Presenting D-E-A-F.* Any effort to describe the remedy would require volumes and volumes of books, which nobody would read. Therefore, we must make movies so there will be more effective activists and the like.

Luczak: How did you hook up with the Mosdeux folks? What made you decide to make this particular film?

Commerson: Wayne Betts, Jr., one of the two co-founders of Mosdeux [a Deaf-owned film studio], was in the same class with me under Facundo Montenegro, one of the best professors Gallaudet has ever seen, bar none. We produced short films for classes and named our student "company" MOS Productions, which incidentally and coincidentally led to the creation of Mosdeux and MOS International at the same time. Quite a coincidence.

I was a graduate student in the Cultural Studies and had to complete a thesis in order to receive a Masters degree. I asked my professor and advisor, Dr. Dirksen Bauman, if I could "write" my thesis in ASL so it wouldn't be shelved like other theses. That's when Wayne Betts, Jr. came in; he shot and edited the film. I wanted the entire world to have access to my thesis. Anyway, after ten years of searching for an answer to significantly transform the Deaf Education, legal and medical systems concerning the Deaf, and after being involved with both protests (Michigan, 2005 and Gallaudet, 2006), I understood that the answer lay in a medium that has had a staying power in shaping of the American culture: film and television programming.

The current ideology says: if you don't speak or hear English well in America, you'll never succeed. Simple. Its simplicity was so profound that everything suddenly seemed ridiculous. Now, what makes ideology an ideology? Everyone needs to have a "shared knowledge" of the values—nobody would disagree that you must know English in this country to be successful. If we can create a new body of knowledge and share it with everyone then what happens to the ideology? It'll shift. It did for the blacks, gays, and women—it was a no-brainer.

HAND-WROUGHT

DEBORAH M. BLUMENSON, PH.D.
Art Historian and Author

Even though I'd met Deborah M. Blumenson (formerly known as Deborah M. Sonnenstrahl) in passing while a student at Gallaudet University during the 1980s, I became more in awe of her accomplishments with her book *Deaf Artists in America: Colonial to Contemporary* (DawnSign Press), the first comprehensive look at Deaf artists in this country.

Raymond Luczak: Can you tell us about your background?

Deborah M. Blumenson, Ph.D.: I came from a culturally oriented background in Baltimore, MD. Despite my physician father's destitute roots (he was one of eight children whose parents emigrated from Poland), they enjoyed arts, music, and theater. My father could play the flute. When they discovered that their newborn daughter was deaf, they vowed that I would not be deprived of what life has to offer. They had no knowledge of sign language so my mother would mouth the words spoken onstage or by a docent at a museum. Granted, it was a burdensome process and I got perhaps 45 percent of what was going on. I even took ballet (four years from the age of seven to 11) and piano lessons (one year at the age of 12) until I rebelled much to my parents' disappointment.

I did not appreciate their efforts until I became a young adult when I enrolled at Gallaudet University, and that is where I learned sign language at the age of 18 in 1954! For the first time in my life I was completely immersed in a signing environment and soon learned to appreciate the beauty, creativity, and picturesqueness of the language.

I had grown up in a rather crowded (my parents, grandparents, great-aunt, and younger brother; two older brothers had passed away prior to be birth) and strict (when education was concerned) yet loving household with a hearing family. My parents had an aversion against ASL as my mother corresponded with the John Tracy Clinic in California who implanted these mottos: "Talk to your child! Never use gestures! Never use your hands or arms! Talk! Talk!" My parents refused to enroll me at the Maryland School for the Deaf since sign language was used. I went to a day school for handicapped children (William S. Baer School) for seven years. Then I was transferred to a very progressive school, The Park School, where I was the only Deaf student at eighth grade. I graduated from this school. Before my mother passed away (my father had died at the age of 58 years so my mother had outlived him by 30 years), she became filled with remorse that she did not learn ASL as she had come to terms with the fact that ASL was my natural language and comfort zone.

Luczak: What were your formative experiences with art like? What convinced you to pursue art as a living?

Blumenson: In addition to my ballet and piano lessons my parents enrolled me in an art school approximately at the age of nine for two years. I enjoyed this form of art since I did not need to hear to make art. Ballet and piano are sound-based arts. I finally could focus on my own innate feelings instead of following the music. I no longer felt like a puppet! In retrospect, I think it was the beginning of my future without being cognizant of it. I even still have a small ceramic duck I made in 1944! However, I knew I would not be an artist *per se* as drawing did not come easily to me as compared with my classmates who drew or paint effortlessly much to my dismay. More than once the art teacher had to lend her helping hand to make my duck more presentable and identifiable.

To be honest, making art as my profession never entered my mind as it was so far-fetched. I owe my choice of career to Mrs. Elva Loe who changed my professional life. Loe taught Art History during my Gallaudet years. When she discovered that I signed up denoting English as major prior to my junior year, she beckoned me to her office. I was making a serious mistake, scolded Mrs. Loe. Judging from my quizzes and test papers, she said I belong to the arts, specifically Art History. Since Art History was not a major at the college during the 1950s, she advised me to major in Art. When I protested that I did not have the flair for drawing and painting she said flatly, "You can learn! It will be beneficial to you because you will better understand the materials and tools they use and also the struggles to get an image from their heads to create a concrete work of art. Moreover, you can always go for your Masters' in Art History." (What a vote of confidence, I thought to myself). I quickly changed my major and never looked back. Granted it were my parents who had instilled the foundation of art appreciation in my innate existence.

Luczak: At what point did you start thinking about Deaf artists? Why?

Blumenson: During my long teaching tenure at Gallaudet (32 years beginning in 1965), my students frequently asked if there were any Deaf artists. It was a wake-up call. The first known Deaf artist was Quintus Pedius who was born deaf during the height of the Roman Empire! Pliny the Elder (23-79 A.D.), a Roman writer and encyclopedist, considered Pedius one of the most eminent painters of ancient Rome! The students' jaws dropped to the floor. I knew this pitiful ignorance had to be resolved. The result? We held, perhaps the first art exhibition of Deaf artists, *Spotlight on Deaf Artists*, in the fall of 1981 at Gallaudet University which featured Deaf artists from bygone years. It was so successful that a second exhibition was established featuring living Deaf artists two years later in 1983. These two exhibitions may have acted as a catalyst for numerous Deaf artists exhibitions which followed including the first Deaf Way Art Festival which showcased approximately 5,000 Deaf artists from the four corners of the world at Gallaudet University in 1989.

Luczak: What was it like to learn in-depth about art as part of your postsecondary studies? How did your thinking about art change?

Blumenson: It was a mind-blowing experience I had when I learned more than what it seemed to be on the surface of an artwork. Due to communication difficulties between the art teacher and yours truly in the art school during my youth, I had not absorbed the nuances of art terms, or even knew that such common physical characteristics including, but not limited to two- or three-dimensional, texture, balance, composition, value, hue, and perspective existed. I was so naïve that I thought all you need is a God-given talent in art, and nothing else mattered. My thinking about art changed when I had to take a required course, Art History, during my freshmen and sophomore years. My observations went through a drastic change. Instead of looking at a work of art at face value, my mind automatically went into an analytic mode utilizing art terms learned in classes. I have seen beautifully executed artwork without taking the aforementioned art terms into consideration. They are not art! Or so I thought. My pedantic analysis has softened lately as art, in general, has stepped out of the proverbial box. However, one characteristic remains and that is the art must convey a message or rather have a story to tell in a most captivating way.

Luczak: Tell us a bit about how your book *Deaf Artists in America: Colonial to Contemporary* came about. What were some of the challenges you've had to deal with? What were some of the more surprising reactions you've gotten for your book?

Blumenson: During my teaching tenure at Gallaudet University, I was approached by Joe Dannis, the owner/publisher of the DawnSignPress to write a book on Deaf artists. I had written and published several articles periodically regarding Deaf artists and museum accessibility but never a book. I knew there was a crucial need for the book as there was no such book on the market. While we were clamoring for Deaf artists to be recognized, what better way to give them clout than a well-respected book? However, I doubted that I was the right person to undertake such a daunting project. I get antsy when sitting too long and could not fathom myself chained to my computer day and night. It was not until I retired from teaching in 1996 when I caved in, and the work for the book became my life 24/7 for the next six years. There were numerous challenges, but my biggest fear was playing "God" as I had no prototype to use as a resource or guideline.

Who was I to accept or reject the inclusion of so many deserving Deaf artists? (Including all Deaf artists would take volumes). Who was I to decide their rightful place in history for prosperity? Who was I to decide their fate? Who was

I to write such a much-needed book? I had numerous sleepless nights and hurdles to clear. Another challenge I had to encounter is deciding the type of readers. Should the book be geared to art students, or general students or serious adults who appreciated art? I had to decide whether to include international artists as well as American artists. Since there was no historical document on Deaf artists regarding their positions in the context of their style, influence, and history, I had to decide whether to list them alphabetically or chronologically. It was not until three months later from Day One when a light bulb flashed in my head. I developed guidelines that produced long-sought answers. It was full steam ahead until the publication of the book.

The most crucial and important surprising reaction to my book was the readers did not realize that there were numerous Deaf artists whose works are featured in the prestigious museums. They would say, "Yes, I know this artist, but did not know he was deaf!" Too often, unfortunately, their deafness was not acknowledged in the museum realm.

I myself had a surprising reaction when one Deaf reader approached me with an empty wine bottle under her arm at a museum where I gave a presentation. I was autographing my book when she abruptly gave me the bottle. I quickly recognized the label as it had an artwork by one of the artists (John Brewster) featured in my book. She signed to me, "Look how famous he is! He was born in 1766!" I was struck with the realization that people in general were beginning to realize that Deaf artists do have a place in the sun. She thanked me profusely for producing such a book.

Luczak: You were there when a group of Deaf artists created the De'VIA statement at the first Deaf Way. In the years since, have you found the De'VIA statement to be still valid, or do you find that the Deaf artist community's output has diverged from that? If so, why do you think that is?

Blumenson: It may appear that people forget that not all Deaf artists are De'VIA artists since the establishment of the De'VIA manifesto in 1989. For instance, during the late nineteenth century, when Claude Monet, a French painter (1840-1926), intentionally or unintentionally started the Impressionism movement, not all his contemporary artists were dabbling in the Impressionist style. Similarly, the trend continues today as we see dual art movements in the deaf world: De'VIA artists and deaf artists who happen to be deaf. We have deaf artists who have no ties with the De'VIA movement and have no intention of making their deafness public. With the advancement of technology, the increasing use of cochlear implants, implementation of mainstream programs, and deaf people rights laws passed by the Congress, we might not see as much De'VIA art today as compared with previous years. Deaf people have become politically savvy and powerfully organized so that the motivation to create De'VIA art may be less urgent. Yet there is an undying need to preserve Deaf culture and that is where De'VIA comes in. However, the characteristics are slowly evolving from negativism to positivism with justified pride and self-esteem. There are continuous De'VIA art exhibitions today. In summary, the urge to preserve Deaf culture may be the catalyst of the continuing survival of De'VIA artists.

Luczak: Where do you see the Deaf artist community going—in a loosely general sense, of course—in terms of their output?

Blumenson: Gone are the days of rote and discipline of subject matter. I see a greater degree of freedom in terms of expression and creativity. Deaf artists have become more aware of their unique world when one does not hear at all or hears imperfectly. They have a wider gamut of subject matter ranging from their actual to emotional world. They have become savvy in technology, and I see a trend in computer/graphics art. The bottom line is they have more confidence trusting themselves to bare their opinions, thoughts, perceptions, and souls, and reach for the sky.

ROBERT WITTIG
Painter

Through an emailing list I was on, I first came across Robert Wittig's web site and discovered that he was a ASL-using Deaf artist living in Chicago.

Raymond Luczak: What led you to become an artist? What situation led you specifically down that path?

Robert Wittig: Deafness, and a stroke. Until June 1994, I was a hearing person, and had just about zero knowledge of either deafness or Deafness. On Memorial Day weekend, 1994, I had a severe stroke that left me deaf, along with a lot of other physical, mental and emotional problems as well. I was almost unable to communicate because of aphasia (an impairment of the ability to use or comprehend words), and I was in a hospital for much of the following year. Eventually, the doctors decided that I was never going to improve any more, so they sent me home, and I went on SSDI as permanently disabled.

Prior to my stroke, I was a furniture finisher, and owned my own small business. The business had to be closed and the factory sold to pay bills, and in January 1996, I got tired of cleaning the house and watching TV I didn't understand, so I went down into the basement, and got out my old furniture painting tools, and began messing around on scraps of wood, and on the backs of canvases that people threw out in the alleys around my house, where my dog liked to walk me.

My left hand was weak, so I got some clay to mess with, figuring it would help my hand (eventually, I learned to use my right hand as my dominant hand), and my first real works were in terra cotta clay, but after I got my hands working a little better, I stopped with the clay, and returned to painting, and have been painting and drawing ever since.

Luczak: What kind of deafness do you have? And how did you learn ASL?

Wittig: My ears are okay, but the paths in my brain that transmit the signals for sound were destroyed by the stroke.

Arthur Tomlinson, a Certified Deaf Interpreter who lives about a mile from my house, who, in addition to knowing several different sign languages, is skilled at communicating with "home signers" and Deaf who had never properly acquired language when they were children. Arthur found me one day, and was the first person I was actually able to understand, in years. He was my first ASL teacher, and introduced me into the Deaf community, where I had many other teachers, who were not professional teachers at all, but who took the time to help me out, one sign at a time, and still do.

I consider ASL my "first" language, because it was not until after I learned ASL well enough to communicate again, that I was able to put my mind to relearning English again, which was my birth language.

ASL is so "everyday" to me that I don't really think about it, and painting is also so "everyday" that I don't think about that much, either. I don't think that ASL plays much of a part in painting, or vice versa; they are two totally different ways to communicate—ASL being a "reasoning language, and painting being a more emotional way of communicating, so that there is almost no overlap between the two, except when I get recruited to draw hand shapes for posters and flyers, for upcoming events.

Luczak: What medium do you work in as a painter? Can you explain something about gouache? Why do you work in that medium?

Wittig: I work in oil, acrylic, watercolor, gouache, pen, ink, pencil, charcoal, pastel (dry and oil), wood, terra cotta, found objects, and anything I can lay hands on.

Gouache is just watercolor with an opaque white added, so that you have opaque color, the way oil paint is, instead of translucent color, which is what watercolor is. I enjoy combining watercolor and gouache in the same painting—using watercolor for things like sky, and water, and gouache for things that I want to be more "solid," like land, buildings, etc. In my opinion, this gives me the best of both worlds—the "airiness" of watercolor and the solidity of oil, in a single, fast-drying painting.

Luczak: What have you learned from using ASL?

Wittig: Before my stroke, I thought I understood human nature, but I did not. When I became deaf, friends I thought were for a lifetime, disappeared in a matter of weeks. At first, I was bitter, then I was depressed, then I met up with some Deafies, made some new friends, figured out I could paint, and learn, and study, and get my life back—not my "old life" but a totally new life—so I quit feeling sorry for myself, and got on with the business of living. I eventually got involved with the Anixter Center here in Chicago, teaching a class in basic computing skills for Deaf adults, and working with Addiction Recovery for the Deaf (ARD).

So, what have I learned?

People are people—Deaf or Hearing. Time is the only really non-renewable resource that we have. You only get to use each minute once, and when they are all used up . . . poof, you're gone. Money is only worth what it is applied to; if you use it to destroy yourself, it is a liability, and even if used wisely, it can't purchase you any extra minutes, once your clock has run down.

I don't know whether my work will ever make much of a difference in the human condition. It is just another grain of sand or two on the beach. The best I can do is to make sure that the work is as honest as possible, and the best I can do. If I can make this so, then I have used my time to the best of my ability, and life cannot ask more than that of a person.

Somewhere over the last few years, I think I went from "deaf" to "Deaf." I stopped looking at deafness as a pathology and a deficit, and began to realize that it is just another way of experiencing existence, and that, like money, it can be a good thing or a bad thing, depending on the individual's attitude.

ANDRÉ PELLERIN
Potter and Ceramicist

When I met André Pellerin in 1985, he was working as the Assistant Technical Director for the Gallaudet University's Theater Arts Department; he had graduated from the Austine School for the Deaf in Brattleboro, Vermont. Like most people, I was fascinated by the idea of having a deafblind person working in theater, but I was more impressed by how thoroughly he knew what he was doing. Then, a few years ago, he discovered pottery, which eventually led to his new job at Gallaudet's Art Department.

Raymond Luczak: How did you end up working in theater?

André Pellerin: Psychology was my major, but I added theater as a production/performance major before I graduated from Gallaudet in December 1982. Originally I had wanted to major in Art but I was told that I should not do that due to my Usher syndrome [a genetic form of deaf-blindness], but I went ahead and added theater as my second major. I had been taking theater courses, which gave me enough credits to finish up my theater major. It was the sceneshop work that I loved—building the sets on stage. I eventually got involved more and more with different technical things, and then I trained crews building the sets and doing runthroughs. I worked very hard to get where I wanted to be at the theater arts department and held that job for twenty-plus years.

Luczak: So what did you learn from your years in theater?

Pellerin: I learned to be true to myself, and that anybody can do what they want, not what others want you to do. About six years ago, I got into my first pottery class under Linda Jordan. I had wanted to do pottery on the wheel for as long as I can remember, but I could not get a chance to do it until I saw the email announcement about Linda's non-credit wheel pottery class. In my first class Linda showed us what we needed to do. Then I sat at the wheel. When I first put my hand on that wet clay, I felt a click in the back of my head and I knew instantly that pottery would be my next big thing in my life. The creative flow came out of me into my hands and to the clay. It wasn't awkward at all. I often feel I've done this in a past life or something.

I started making small bowls first. Then I began going to the pottery studio during my lunch hour and after work to make more and more. I had to practice and practice to get to where I am now. I screwed up quite a few times in the beginning. I wasn't the only one who screwed up. We all laughed together.

But at first, the wheel was a bit boring. I had to wedge the clay to make sure there was no air inside before using it on the wheel. If there is air in the clay and you put it in the kiln to fire it, the clay will explode. Then I had to learn how to center it. Otherwise, one side of the bowl will be thicker than the other side.

Luczak: So how do you get the air out?

Pellerin: When you throw the clay on the wheel—when I say "throw," I mean a method of bringing up the clay onto the wheel—you can feel bumps, almost like blisters. Usually they have air there. I wedge the clay in such a way to take the air out, and then I cut it in half with a wire to see if there are any holes. If you throw it right, there are no holes.

Once I got the hang of it, I got so much better. I'm now making huge pots, bowls and jars. When I say "huge," I mean big—about two feet high and 14 to 18 inches wide. I try to make jars taller every time I make a new one. I always learn new methods when I make new pots. I don't make all my pots the same. I make the same pots again and again until I get sick of it before trying new shapes and sizes. It's a challenge.

Luczak: Do you learn anything from showing your work to other people?

Pellerin: I try to do things the way I want them to look because it reflects me. The good part is that what I make that pleases me seems to please others. I guess I'm lucky. I did an art show with about 110 pieces last year. People said that when they went into that gallery at the Washburn Arts Building, they could see that I was very happy with what I do. My work was colorful and easy on their eyes, and the flow of the room was like the flow of a river. I guess that was because when I was setting up my exhibit, I felt very peaceful and in my own world, so when I finally opened that door, it was like opening myself up to everyone at my exhibit.

NANCY CREIGHTON
Graphic Designer

Over twenty years ago at Gallaudet, I met the lovely Nancy Creighton. When I learned that she'd moved to Philadelphia, I had to follow up.

Raymond Luczak: What do you remember most about your artistic aspirations while growing up?

Nancy Creighton: My mother was artistic in an amateur way. She loved to sing and draw. She encouraged my drawing and painting experiments as well as my dancing. Dad didn't have any artistic leanings at all. But he loved me and wanted me to do what made me happy. They never expected much to come from it. I was really raised as "poor little Nancy who can't hear. We hope she grows up to find a good man to marry who'll take care of her." It was the '50s and '60s. That I'd grow up to be a self-sufficient deaf woman artist never entered my parents' minds.

I started taking dance lessons at the age of five. Not only because I enjoyed it, but I came to understand much later that dancing was one of the things that my mother thought it would help me develop my residual hearing.

Much later, when I decided to learn sign language, there was a poster of dancers on the wall of the Deaf Community Center. I took the poster down off the bulletin board and read it—it was really a newsletter from Spectrum, *Focus on Deaf Artists*, and the article was about the Spectrum Deaf Dance Company. A few months later, I moved to Austin—no friends, no income, just a desire to join the dance company. I'd been signing for less than a year, so communication was iffy, too.

Spectrum was my real entry into the world of Deaf people—my own world at last. I was with the dance company for about a year, when I had a falling-out with the artistic director and left the company. Once I stopped performing, I focused on my visual arts skills.

Luczak: How did Purple Swirl Arts come about?

Creighton: I started the company while I was working full-time at the National Association of the Deaf (NAD) as a way of keeping up with my artistic roots. When I started at NAD, I was "Ms. Broadcaster," which was CEO Nancy J. Bloch's teasing term. I was doing almost everything myself—with guidance and support from the NAD staff. "Everything" meant all editing, layout and design work; creating ads for NAD; and selling advertising space in *The NAD Broadcaster*.

This was exciting, demanding and satisfying because I was stretching my creative side in new directions, and developing more analytical skills at the same time. In 1996, when the World Wide Web was still fairly new, NAD entered the online world with its first web site. I was the point person working with an outside designer. She then taught me how to maintain the site. This meant I was working on two publications—print and web—and it became too much for one person to handle.

My job began to shift toward site maintenance and management. As I became more involved with its management, I needed a creative outlet. With Purple Swirl Arts, I got involved with the Cafepress online store and the business card online studio. I had been looking for a way to get my designs out into the world. In the same way that I needed to perform in order to dance, I needed to see my artwork on something other than just on my computer screen or dot-matrix color printouts to feel satisfaction as an artist.

My first design for the store was a blue heart, which I put it on a shirt and gave it to a friend. The online store just grew from there. I soon discovered Printing Automation for business cards. I love their cards as their print work is outstanding. I started doing my own designs and posting them on my site.

Luczak: Tell me about the latest project you've done for NAD. What did you learn from the process?

Creighton: Persistence! I'd worked on books before, but working with Larry Newman, the author of *Sands of Time: NAD Presidents 1880-2003*, I learned the meaning of persistence all over again. Larry "finished" his book and sent it to NAD to be published. But we saw his book as a good first draft. I worked with him on revisions to the book while I was at NAD, but NAD is not just a publishing company. It was difficult to devote time to it regularly. Larry was a "good nagger"—he constantly pushed me along whenever he hadn't heard back from me about the most recent revisions.

When I left NAD to move to Philadelphia, I completed the book as a freelancer. I was finally able to devote my time to this, and the book was unveiled at the recent NAD Conference. All of the living presidents were there together onstage. It was a marvelous introduction to the history of Deaf people, told through the stories of the men and women who have led NAD.

ANNA AND SEAN VIRNIG
Industrial Designers

Every month I've always featured someone from the arts community, but it occurred to me that industrial design is also an art form. I thought immediately of Anna and Sean Virnig of Rawland Cycles. I was particularly impressed with how much they'd focused on not producing just another bicycle.

Raymond Luczak: Could you tell us a bit about your background?

Anna & Sean Virnig: Proud alumni of the California School for the Deaf, Fremont (CSDF) and Gallaudet University, we live in a quaint liberal riverfront town of Northfield, Minnesota where we raise our children and operate Rawland among many other things typical for a young family. Initially I grew up in Minnesota and attended the Minnesota State Academy for the Deaf and public schools in Faribault. Anna hailed from Hanford, California when she transferred to CSDF. Interestingly enough, we missed each other by a summer when I enrolled at CSDF after her graduation. That was how we had the same teachers and friends. After graduating from Gallaudet, we traveled Europe together for three months before moving to Minnesota. During our stay in Europe, besides watching a Formula 1 race in Spain and visiting countless museums, we walked up the Alpe d' Huez in France where we saw several of Tour de France's greatest in action. Anna was hooked for life. We then visited DeRosa, a legendary old-world bicycle factory in Milan, Italy. Little did we know we would be into bicycle business ten years later.

Luczak: How did you get involved with biking?

Virnig: I knew I was hooked from the very moment my dad gave me a single, powerful shove from the behind on my first ride on a maroon Huffy sans training wheels in 1978. Anna was gravitated toward the fascinating world of cycling subculture that pretty much parallels that of Deaf culture. Suffice it to say, the rest took its course. The Deaf and cycling communities are strikingly similar in many respects, with regard to art, legal rights, technology, history, and so on. For example, trends in the cycling industry ebb and flow just like education and technology trends in the Deaf community. There is a pattern to that, so we knew we got into the bicycle business at an opportune time when people begin to realize the intrinsic value of owning a versatile bicycle for riding road and dirt and pretty much everything else in between. We would fancy Rawland as the ASL of bicycles, with reverence for the natural transmission for visceral activities that are riding and signing, respectively.

Luczak: When did you realize that a bicycle could be a work of art?

Virnig: Right before riding for the first time at age five, my dad pointed out that my maroon Huffy had a chrome fork of a certain design I still like today. In my opinion, bicycle is a perfect symbiosis of harmony created by art and engineering, both human ingenuities infused with passion. Like art, intuition takes over when Anna and I look at bicycles. This reminds us of the first couple pages of Malcolm Gladwell's *Blink: The Power of Thinking Without Thinking*. After starting up Rawland, we could tell pretty soon whether a bicycle looks, feels, and rides right by simply glancing at it. There are certain things we look for such as rider position, tire clearance, wheel size, tire type, frame and fork dimensions and proportions, and components that makes up the bicycle and the rider as a synergistic whole.

Luczak: Why did you set up Rawland? Why that name?

Virnig: Rawland is an English translation of my mother's Norwegian surname. The name is also an accurate portrayal of Rawland's versatile design philosophy. Imagine a Subaru with Porsche handling. This concept was deemed too radical when I discussed with custom bicycle framebuilders for my own use, for there was no such bicycle. So, starting up Rawland was just a natural thing to do, if not logical. Now we have customers telling us that Rawland is just what they have been looking for all along.

Luczak: Are most of the people you work with on your Rawland bicycles non-signers?

Virnig: Very much so. Technology levels the playing field. Meeting my retailers and customers in person at international trade shows momentarily presented a challenge. Many, especially those from other countries, were not accustomed to working with interpreters, let alone a Deaf person. Soon enough they liked what they saw in my booth, so that made things much easier. However, some of them were testy at first by peppering me with technical questions. I expected that, and was able to validate my design elements by simply pointing at unique features on Rawland bicycles. Seeing was indeed believing in this instance.

Luczak: How do you work with designers on Rawland bicycles?

Virnig: As the initial designer, I had all the elements ready beforehand. And then Anna and I wondered how we could communicate our vision for Rawland products to our designer with an established reputation and international contacts in the bicycle industry. We soon realized that the elements already took care of that; he understood right away what we wanted to achieve. Although I do not have formal training in design and engineering, my 30 years of experience helped me a great deal in this regard. Rawland is increasingly revered for its geometry in the blogsphere and elsewhere. That is something I am especially proud of, for this is the Holy Grail for every bicycle design. Once the desired geometry is achieved, then this resonates to everything else. Only a handful of bicycles I have ridden can attest to that. Rawland also features many design details that sets it apart from many other bicycles, its competitors included. That makes Rawland ideal for commuting, touring, racing, and so on, all with one design platform, just like what Subaru, the automotive equivalent of Rawland, does to its lineup. Most of their models share the same chassis, engine, and so on. I would characterize that as platform proliferation for all the right reasons.

BRIAN SELZNICK
Illustrator and Writer

When I read Brian Selznick's novel *The Invention of Hugo Cabret*, which the director Martin Scorsese has turned into a fantastic movie called *Hugo*, I was blown away. But his next novel *Wonderstruck* featured two Deaf people as the main characters. I had to find out more about Mr. Selznick!

Raymond Luczak: Could you please tell us a bit about your growing up years, and what led you to the world of book illustration?

Brian Selznick: I grew up the oldest of three children in East Brunswick, NJ. It was a lovely suburban community with a great art program in the public schools. I went to camp in the summers and loved drawing and making art most of all. My grandmother had a maid who gave me tin foil when I was very small so I could make sculptures. In kindergarten my report card said that I was a good artist. I was told in high school that I should illustrate children's books, and that made me not want to illustrate children's books. It wasn't until I'd graduated college and decided against a career in stage design that I realized my love of art, writing and kids probably meant I should, in fact, be making children's books. I got a job at a children's bookstore in the early nineties called Eeyore's Books for Children and my first book, *The Houdini Box*, was published while I was working there. I left the store six months later, and I've been making books ever since.

Luczak: It seems *The Invention of Hugo Cabret* was a turning point for you, correct?

Selznick: Every time I make a book my goal for myself is to make it better than the last book I made. By the time I made *Hugo* I'd written or illustrated over 20 books for children and I'd learned a lot about storytelling and visual narratives. One thing that frustrated me though, was the fact that most novels for older kids don't include narrative illustrations (pictures that advance the plot). If a novel has pictures, it's usually either small "spot" illustrations that show an interesting moment, or single page illustrations that highlight something important. If you removed the pictures from most novels for older readers, you'd still be able to perfectly understand the story. With *Hugo* I had the idea to try to tell the story like a movie, since the book has much to do with the history of cinema. I removed text and created narrative visual sequences to advance the plot and are imperative to understanding the full narrative. This was something I'd never done before and I loved the challenge of creating a book like this. I learned a lot about the connection between the cinema and picture books, and loved making sequences that mimicked panning shots, edits, zooms and other camera tricks. I loved how people embraced the idea of reading the pictures as well as reading the words. Pictures are usually taken for granted and the importance is given to the text, but with *Hugo* the importance was spread evenly between the two.

Luczak: How did *Wonderstruck* come about?

Selznick: When I was making *Hugo*, I happened to catch a PBS documentary called *Through Deaf Eyes*, which was about the history of Deaf culture and education. Two things struck me as particularly interesting in this documentary. One was an interview with a young deaf man who had grown up in a hearing household. His parents were great and taught him to sign, but it wasn't until he went to college and met other Deaf people that he realized he was part of a larger community. That idea of finding a community and a culture outside of your biological family fascinated me. There was also a section on the transition from silent movies to sound in 1927. The narrator said this was a tragedy for the Deaf community because for the first time they couldn't enjoy the same movies as their hearing counterparts. As a hearing person, I'd never thought about this from the point of view of the Deaf before. There was also a quote from the Deaf educator George Veditz in 1910 who had said that the Deaf were "the people of the eye."

After I finished *Hugo* and was trying to figure out what to do next, I thought it might be interesting to separate the words and the pictures and tell two different stories in one book. But I needed a reason to tell a story with pictures (the reason for the pictures in *Hugo* was the link to the cinema). I remembered the documentary and the quote from George Veditz, and thought it might be interesting to tell the story of a deaf character just with pictures so that we experience her story in a way that reflects how she might experience her own life. The story grew from there.

By coincidence, my boyfriend David Serlin, who is a professor at the University of California, San Diego, works with two of the leading Deaf scholars in the country, Carol Padden and Tom Humphries. They are friends of ours now, and Carol and Tom were incredibly generous with their time and their expertise. They read my manuscript many times to make sure my references to Deaf history were accurate, and they also helped me make sure that my descriptions of the experience of being deaf was rendered as accurately as possible. I also interviewed a few other Deaf people, and I read many books on the subject. I am of course aware that no single member of a community can speak for that entire community, but having the opportunity to discuss issues and plot-related questions with people like Carol and Tom at least let me know that the work I was doing seemed to be heading in the right direction.

I was fascinated to discover many details, like the connection between the history of Deaf education and the history of printing (since deaf people are not bothered by the loud machines, young Deaf men were trained for many years as printers, a detail that went into my book). Carol and Tom helped me understand how sign language, with its own grammar and rules, has a rich and intriguing history and is constantly evolving like any living language. I was also very interested in exploring issues of communication in the book. There are scenes with a Deaf character who signs, a deaf character who doesn't sign but who can speak, and a hearing character who can sign. Figuring out how all these characters communicate with each other in a realistic way was very challenging, but Carol and Tom pointed the way.

Luczak: Your first reading for *Wonderstruck* was ASL-interpreted. That surprised me; most bookstores don't have the budget for interpreters for their readings. How did that come about?

Selznick: I asked Scholastic to contact all the people hosting me on my tour to encourage them to bring in sign interpreters for my talks. I'm writing this to you from Kansas City and so far in the last two and a half weeks I've been in New York, New Jersey, Pennsylvania, Washington, D.C., Toronto and Chicago, and I'd say that the majority of all the events have brought in interpreters. As a hearing person, it's a pleasure to be interpreted. I usually speak fast and use my hands a lot, and having a sign interpreter standing next to me reminds me to slow down, which makes me more considerate of what I'm saying. I also try to use my hands less, so it's not distracting. This calms me down a bit too. I'm trying to learn sign myself, but I'm very slow. So far the only full sentences I know are "Nice to meet you," and "I need to learn sign." Well, it's a start.

BEX FREUND
Painter and Cartoonist

I first saw Bex Freund in a fantastic online clip entitled *Talking Art with Bex*, but I had no idea that I would end up spending a month with her as part of the Deaf Artists Residency Program at the Anderson Center for Interdisciplinary Arts outside Red Wing, Minnesota. She was there to develop her graphic novel-in-progress.

Raymond Luczak: What do you typically tell other Deaf people about your background when you meet them for the first time?

Bex Freund: I don't typically share too many details about myself. It typically depends on the context of our meeting and how I know them. Most of the time, I only divulge that I am a painter and cartoonist based in the San Francisco Bay Area.

Luczak: How did you get into art? What sort of things did you typically draw/make?

Freund: I have always made art. Even as a prelinguistic toddler, I spent hours just drawing. As I got older, it was a typical routine to sit at the kitchen counter with a tall stack of blank paper and a pen, furiously drawing monsters and animals and dinosaurs for hours. Too often, I broke the pen nib, so I usually had extras. In first grade, when asked what I wanted to be when I grew up, my answer was always, "A famous painter." When I graduated from middle school, I enrolled in a magnet high school for the arts. That's when I started to really find my voice and develop the seeds of the stories that became my current graphic novel project, *Fever-Dreams of the City that Never Was*.

Going to art high school was a huge transformation. I went from being in a small bubble of the same Deaf peers that I'd known since kindergarten to suddenly being the only Deaf person in my entire high school. Coping was very difficult at first. I had a lot of issues. I had to learn how to interact with hearing people that weren't members of my family—it was a completely different ball game. The hours were longer than a normal school—we didn't get out until 4 p.m., and we had eleven classes per semester. It was really intense, and more like college than anything else. Even our buildings were leased from within a major college campus, so it wasn't like a typical high school campus. All of the people in the school were once that one weird artsy kid in the corner of the class—so to be in an entire school of people like myself was something quite remarkable, and it went a long way toward figuring myself out as a person and what kind of art I wanted to do.

Luczak: You're in art college now. Is it different from high school?

Freund: I am currently enrolled in the MFA in Comics program at California College of the Arts (CCA). I also went to CCA as an undergrad. The experience of arts high school and undergraduate arts weren't too different, but graduate school is something else altogether. My field of study is now intensely concentrated, like a laser beam, on comics. Before that, I'd always explored a broad range of mediums—writing, illustration, poetry, painting, some sculpture, and photography. But comics takes all of those elements and distills it into something else altogether, and with its own language and rules.

Luczak: When did you start painting? How do you typically approach the creation of a painting?

Freund: I've been painting for as long as I can remember, almost as long as I've been drawing. I started learning oils when I was about seven or eight, and I've remained mostly loyal to that medium ever since. Painting isn't very formal for me. I generally start out with a concept or image in mind, and then just jump right into it. It's a dance, and I always try to have fun.

Luczak: Who are some of your favorite artists? How have they affected or inspired you?

Freund: It's hard to define or articulate how exactly certain artists affect and inspire me. It's beyond anything mere words can encapsulate. I especially love Jenny Saville, Francis Bacon, Ralph Steadman, Zdzisław Beksiński, and Irving Norman.

Luczak: Do you think ASL has had an impact on your artwork itself, or do you feel that it's more about your view of the world? Or is it more about your experience as a Deaf person?

Freund: The short answer is no. The longer, more complex answer is this: To the extent that my deafness has shaped my life experiences and worldview, it's unavoidable, because I can't clinically separate myself from my art—however, my art is not about deafness or Deafhood, and I've never directly addressed such themes in my work. In regard to certain cases of self-portraiture, there are themes such as isolation that do have a history of being in other Deaf artists' work as well. It's a specific kind of isolation—not the universal, generic sort, but one that stems from a language barrier and lack of comprehension on hearing people's parts—they might relate to what I have to say, but never have personally experienced it. It's never a message that is deliberately conveyed, but the theme does sometimes organically surface as a consequence of its role in my personal history.

Luczak: I'd love to learn what you hope to achieve with your current graphic novel project.

Freund: "Achieve"? That's an interesting word to use. The only achievement I truly hope for is merely to finish the book itself. It will be the culmination of almost a decade's worth of my brain muttering snatches of stories to itself, making up ideas and dreamscapes and nonsense words and imagery and scraps from my own life that all gradually spun into accretion disks—little particles of dust smashing and welding together, growing planetary-sized. It's an entire universe existing in my head, and I simply want to just drill a hole in my head and pour it all out into a book, and share that with other people.

ROBERT WALKER
Painter

The Internet can be a wonderful way to meet people you've never heard of. When I read a remarkably astute comment posted by a Robert Walker on a mutual friend's Facebook page, I checked out his profile and discovered his wonderful paintings.

Raymond Luczak: So you're based in Arkansas?

Robert Walker: I'm a fifth-generation Arkansan, and my family is hearing. I am the only one who is Deaf. My mother had gotten the rubella contagion, which was rampant at the time, from my older sister. Then I was found to be deaf at the age of three and placed at the Arkansas School for the Deaf (ASD) at five years old. During this period, I was taken to speech therapy; signs were not permitted within the classroom but allowed during recess and outside the classroom. While my family never learned ASL, I did use a mixture of limited speech, gestures and home and ASL signs. My family did not encourage this mode of communication as they wanted to emphasize the oral approach and this was practiced as much as possible. My enrollment at the ASD lasted two and a half years. My parents then placed me in a public school.

This was well before the ADA laws, so there was no support system to meet my needs. I was required to sit in the front and as close to the teacher's desk as possible. How I survived those years, I'll never know. But I managed somehow and gained an excellent grasp of English (both written and oral). It was not until well after high school that I'd fallen back into the Deaf world (having had no contact with the Deaf community for much of my school years). Gradually, I'd more or less picked up where I'd left off from my ASD days and went on from there. I attended the University of Arkansas as Little Rock upon high school graduation, focusing mainly on studio art courses in which I excelled. It was not until I started taking other required classes, such as lectures, English, history, math, etc., when it became extremely difficult to continue. After flunking several of those classes, I discontinued school and went to work for the family business where I remained for years. It was not until after I'd turned 37 that I met with a vocational rehabilitation counselor who encouraged me to return to the university. This time I was provided with note-takers and interpreters. After two years of part-time attendance, I transferred to Gallaudet University where I stayed until my graduation in 2002.

Luczak: What drew you to art? How did that come about?

Walker: Art was my first mode of communication with my family, using my blackboard in my playroom to convey my wants and needs. This was started one day after my mother picked me up from ASD. As always, she asked me carefully, "What did you do today?" That day had been a "big deal" and I was excited about it, but did not have English words to tell her with. Instead, I just sat there restlessly en route home and once there, immediately made for my black board to draw stick figures of children sitting in a group on the floor watching an old-fashioned projector movie. That was the big deal. I kept on drawing and painting after gaining a hold of languages.

Luczak: Why did you leave Washington, D.C.? Do you miss it at all?

Walker: Upon graduation from Gallaudet with a B.A. in graphic design, I had wanted to stay on in the area and tried to find an apartment while searching for work. This proved difficult to achieve due to my lack of employment so when fall came, I decided to return to my hometown in Arkansas. I do miss the wonderful outdoor cafes that dotted the city. The Deaf community there is yet another factor I have missed as well. There was never a lack of events nor was there of well-educated Deaf people with whom I could discuss a variety of issues, especially related to art.

Luczak: What medium(s) do you tend to work in? Why do you paint?

Walker: These days I am focusing on oils. I had worked with watercolors for over 25 years, and spent several years working with acrylics. I also do graphite drawings as well. Why do we breathe? Why do I paint? I must. :-) Art is the core of my life; it's just inside of me. I fully expect to die with a paintbrush in my hand.

Luczak: It seems that animals figure predominantly in your work. Why is that so?

Walker: I feel that animals are a gift to us, in whatever fashion that may take. As being such, I felt that we should respect that and do all that we can to promote this ideal. I find them interesting to work with, not only in the varied physical attributes they all possess, but their individual personalities too. However I enjoy working with people and often try to include them in studies of animals. There is a strong relationship between us and the animal kingdom in all facets of life. I also do De'VIA work and have done well in juried De'VIA shows.

SUE CLANCY
Mixed-Media Artist

For five years now, Sue Clancy has been doing a cartoon strip called *Signs of Life* for *SIGNews*. Imagine my surprise when she told me that wasn't all that she created. Once I checked her portfolio online, I was immediately impressed by her use of mixed media.

Raymond Luczak: Tell me a bit about your artwork beyond your cartoon strip.

Sue Clancy: Much of the humorous images (fine art, illustrations, or cartoons) I create stem from an exploration of words and images and how they intersect in our mind to create meaning. Or you might say, as a result of my deafness. As you know us Deaf, when we aren't in an ASL environment, we rely heavily on the visual world, the colors, the lights, the shapes, the patterns and so on around us to tell us more information than we might have if we only relied on the words we might lipread or see written. Reflecting this, I create visual puzzles for the viewer to piece together a word-story or sense of meaning from its colors, shapes, and patterns. Essentially the viewer of my art can do what, as a deaf person, I do every day. But there is a lot of room for humor here—in that so many words and elements of the visual world have multiple meanings. That's what I like to explore artistically.

A good example of how my deafness can inspire my work is my piece called *Poultry Reading*. Here in Oklahoma people have a way of talking, where words with one syllable will become two- or three-syllable words or words that have multiple syllables turn into words with only one syllable. For example, instead of saying "Po-e-try," they say "Potry," all slurred together so that when you're lipreading the word looks rather similar to the word "Poultry." Lipreading in Oklahoma can be such fun. (Ha!)

Luczak: Can you share something about how you approach your paintings?

Clancy: My paintings are created by using cut pieces of handmade paper. This technique is a physical manifestation of the way the human mind combines and compounds isolated patterns of information into a new conceptual whole. Each paper I find or create starts life as a single handmade sheet. I dye it with a color, stencil a pattern on it, marble it, or block print a design onto its surface, whatever is required to create the necessary patterns for my visual story. Then I cut shapes out of the separate sheets of paper and combine those cut shapes into new ones that are then glued onto a two-inch deep cradled wood panel. This technique creates layers of pattern and shape. There are often several hundreds of cut handmade and patterned paper shapes in each of my paintings. Like elements within a joke every pattern and shape I use individually contributes to the conceptual story. Once the story is constructed out of paper I add a highlight or a shadow using acrylic paint as necessary. The finished painting is varnished. Every paintings story/image continues around the four cradled edges of the panel. Often there is an additional joke on one or more of these edges for the in-person viewer to discover. As a result no matter where one physically stands to view my work there is always more to the story. Looking at it from different angles allows the viewer to truly appreciate the entire painting. My paintings have depth like all good stories.

Luczak: What are you working on these days?

Clancy: I'm currently working on more illustrations for books, magazines—I want to do more work in the publishing field. For instance, my artwork was used as a cover illustration for a book titled *Travelin' Music: A Poetic Tribute to Woody Guthrie* (Village Books Press). Recently United Disability Services's *Kaleidoscope* magazine used one of my artworks as their Christmas card image for the 2010 season. I'm also working on several surface design illustrations that are repeatable images to be used on textiles, gift-wrap paper, or really anywhere an image needs to be repeated in a pattern. Of course it goes without saying that I'd like to do more fine art exhibits. I'm working on a new artwork series just now.

CHARLIE SWINBOURNE
Scribbler

Spending a month in the United Kingdom really opened my eyes to a vibrant British Sign Language (BSL) community. Among them is the Deaf artist and blogger Charlie Swinbourne, who is big on scribbling and has begun selling T-shirts with scribbles on them.

Raymond Luczak: You grew up in a Deaf family. Does that mean you wear hearing aids?

Charlie Swinbourne: My earliest memories are of taking them off—finding them uncomfortable and throwing them on the floor. I even put them down the toilet at one point! My Mum wasn't too happy. But I wear my hearing aids every day while resisting the temptation to throw them down the toilet. I now live in London where I work as a researcher for *See Hear!*, the BBC deaf show.

Luczak: Were you always interested in art while growing up?

Swinbourne: Whenever I visited relatives I'd draw something, animals, cartoon characters or people. It was a way of spending some quiet time while everyone was going mad around me! I had a lot of cousins, and I was the oldest, so I'd start drawing and they'd all soon follow, so there'd be six of us in a line scribbling. Several of my portraits of my cousins now hang on the wall of my auntie's house! So I guess I wasn't too bad. I was also a fan of art at school, and I'd say that certain artists like Jackson Pollock and Vincent Van Gogh influenced me. I liked things that were spontaneous, partly because so many people worry about getting everything just right, so they don't draw anything. That's a mistake. I think there's a value in just moving that pen across the page, no matter what it looks like in the end. Expressing yourself is really important.

Luczak: What's up with your obsession with scribbling?

Swinbourne: It's something that's grown and grown. I first scribbled at primary school all over a workbook that got my teacher very angry. It was all about being different from the crowd and doing something individual. It was also naughty! But that was probably the only naughty thing I did; I was generally a good pupil. But I was also a frustrated one. Where I grew up in the countryside, the only deaf people I knew were my family; I went to a mainstream school. I got by and made lots of hearing friends, but I was always the odd one out. When things got busy in the classroom, I couldn't make out what was going on. I guess I scribbled as an escape into my own little world.

Luczak: You seem to enjoy blogging a lot.

Swinbourne: Starting my blog "The Scribbler" was the first time I started putting all the different things I do into one place. I'd always scribbled as I was doing different things at work or while watching TV. So when I started the blog, I put these little scribbles on there. I think there's about 30 or so on there now, but the blog also has photos and writing on it. Like many deaf people, I'm a visual person so I'd always loved taking photos of anything that looked remotely interesting. So photos of random things went on there.

I realized that while writing letters home from the university, I enjoyed sharing what I'd been up to. Somehow writing seemed to put things into perspective, but I realized I could write in an entertaining way, that I could make people laugh just by reading my writing. I started a column at the university about my life, and it was called "Mr." I didn't realize it at the time, but that column would later lead me into a career in the media, with television and magazines.

Luczak: How did you get the idea for creating scribbled T-shirts?

Swinbourne: Sometimes people asked me if they could keep the little scribbles I did, which surprised me, but I was more than happy to oblige. I felt honored that people saw value in something which represents being free, like a little bit of imagination on the page. Then one day in an arts shop when I was picking up paints (as I sometimes do larger scribbles!), I saw T-shirt paints. I didn't really think they existed, but I bought some with some cheap blank T-shirts.

At first they looked terrible. As I kept going, they improved. One day I wore one myself. People started to ask me where I'd got it from! They'd never seen one quite like that. So I made more, giving them to family and friends at first. I decided to do a bit more—I made a load of T-shirts, each of which was totally unique, and just happened to move in with Sam Dore, a web site designer. We decided to sell our scribbler shirts online. Scribbling's all about not taking life too seriously. Just have fun. Scribble. If I don't sell any T-shirts, I'll still be glad I tried. I can't play music or sing, but I can scribble, and that's what I intend to keep doing.

VANESSA VAUGHAN
Painter and Actress

When I spotted Vanessa Vaughan's name at the Deaf Culture Center in Toronto, Canada, where they were holding an exhibition featuring Deaf female Canadian artists, I had to smile. I had met her years before when I lived in New York. It was time to reconnect with her.

Raymond Luczak: How did your family react to your deafness?

Vanessa Vaughan: At the time my deafness was discovered, my parents tried to get as much information as they could and they were told to teach me to speak and to listen. My parents agreed because they wanted me to learn the language of our community so I could play with the neighborhood children and go to the public school facing our backyard. My parents spent hours drawing with me to communicate where we were going or doing. I was first exposed to sign language when I appeared as a child actor in my first film called *Clown White*, which featured a variety of Deaf children.

Luczak: How did you get involved with acting?

Vaughan: After *Clown White*, which I performed in with a variety of Deaf children at the age of nine, I had a wonderful time with the people on set. There was a strong sense of "family" spirit and I had a feeling that I would be back someday. Years later, while in high school, I co-starred opposite Kiefer Sutherland in *Crazy Moon*. I have continued on from time to time in various films and television shows with my latest appearance being in Sarah Polley's feature *Away from Her*.

Luczak: How did you get involved with art? It seems that you're focusing much more on your art than on your acting career.

Vaughan: I always knew I wanted to be an artist since I was a young child. I consider myself first and foremost a Visual Artist. It is something I could connect with deeply and call my own. I studied specialized art in high school and then continued in university. I now have collectors around the world and exhibit regularly in Muskoka, a popular destination for cottagers that is also the source of inspiration for my landscapes (the unusually colorful skies and reflected color on water). Art, creating and painting—all of what it encompasses—is my passion. Acting is something I fell into and got lucky with many wonderful opportunities and experiences.

Luczak: Tell us about your evolution as an artist, and whether Deafness has influenced your artwork.

Vaughan: It was not until I learned about De'VIA after meeting Brenda Schertz and Lesley Kushner, who had put on a Deaf art exhibit in New York City, that I began to examine my work introspectively to see if my deafness had an impact. I saw that I had some similarities to other Deaf artists such as my vivid use of contrasting color to create movement. It was exciting for me as an artist to discover that I belong to a category of art (such as Surrealism, Impressionism, etc). I noticed however, that my use of color began to change after I got my cochlear implant so I wonder if there was indeed a direct relationship between hearing sound and color, or if it was a pure coincidence as part of my artistic journey. Only time will tell.

PATTI DURR

Arts Advocate and Activist

I was so impressed with NTID's Deaf artists web site that I had to ask its coordinator Patti Durr about it.

Raymond Luczak: Please tell us a bit about your background.

Patti Durr: I was born partially deaf to a hearing family. I attended public schools without any support services except for speech therapy. I never saw another Deaf person until I was 20 years old. I began learning ASL from a community college in Syracuse and went to Gallaudet summer school to learn more ASL.

Luczak: What were your initial experiences with art like?

Durr: As a child I was always attracted to the arts—language arts, theater, and visual art. The first time I saw Deaf-themed visual art was probably at the Deaf Way I conference in 1989. I was a baby in the Deaf world at this time (an adult but only an infant with an emerging Deaf center), but I clearly remember attending the presentation where Betty G Miller announced the De'VIA manifesto, which a small group of Deaf visual artists had created during a week-long workshop before Deaf Way I. I was so intrigued by this new genre and framework. I thought, "*Wow*. This is an formidable moment in history even though the name and I were still in our infancy."

I did not create any Deaf-themed visual art until recently when Paula Grcevic, a Deaf artist, professor, and colleague, invited me to exhibit some work in a show on Mythology Images she was curating for the Dyer Arts Center at NTID. I hesitantly accepted. I had no idea that it would create such a dilemma for me—I was totally stumped—almost like a writer's block I imagine, but for me it was a visual arts block. All my creative works prior have been collective-based; I've worked and weaved together plays and video productions in small groups. I had a horrible time grounding myself. My hearing husband and kids banished me to the basement laundry room where my makeshift studio was set up. I spent hours and hours every night just playing and changing and fretting and finally letting go and letting the art decide what it wanted to be. It was a marvelous experience for me. I truly thank Paula for believing in me more than I did myself.

Luczak: What prompted you to create the Deaf artists web site?

Durr: Long before creating Deaf-themed visual art, I began to formally study De'VIA when I started teaching more Deaf Cultural Studies courses at NTID. Eventually Paula Grcevic asked me to take over the teaching of a course she developed with a hearing art professor at NTID, Barbara Fox, on Deaf Art and Deaf Artists. I initially felt out of my expertise and very intimidated by the large boxes of files and slides Paula handed over to my care. I felt like I was being entrusted with the riches of Deaf culture. I didn't feel worthy; I have no formal training as an artist or an art historian. But Paula's belief in me fueled me forward. My background in sociology helped me find my footing. Paula and Barbara had already created an outstanding and forward-thinking International Archives of Deaf Artists (IADA), which included De'VIA and non-De'VIA artists. Many artists came from the Deaf Artists of America (DAA) collection from Tom Willard. Designed before the age of web-design and by librarians, the site's initial focus was on cataloging rather than having a user-friendly interface. Since the materials were so precious, I worked with a Deaf web designer, Simon Ting, at NTID to make a more easily navigable site. I worked on expanding the site by including articles, videos, and additional resources. Joan Naturale, our Deaf librarian at RIT's Wallace Memorial Library, was instrumental in getting copyright permission for reproducing articles and videos on the site. Cathy Clarke handled the layout and design look of the site. Paula Grcevic continues to assist in evaluating potential artists for the site. However, the site cannot replace the experience of seeing the original works up close and personaldetails, textures, colors.

The site is ideal though for reaching out to the masses and has increased the visibility of many Deaf artists and their works. It's also inspired many emerging Deaf artists and more in-depth examination of De'VIA. With hits from all over the world the site gets a great deal of traffic daily and continues to grow and improve. The site has submission guidelines for new or undiscovered Deaf artists.

Luczak: I've noticed that you seem to be open to including hearing artists.

Durr: The De'VIA manifesto says that Deaf and Hearing people can create De'VIA as long as they manifest the intention to represent the Deaf experience in their work. Presently we have one hearing artist out of over 100 Deaf artists on the site.

De'VIA works in many ways are the heart of Deaf culture—they communicate a wealth of information about our lineage, struggles, hopes, commonalities, differences, language, values, and traditions. In many ways our De'VIA artists, as well as those who create in the air (ASL poets, storytellers, and orators), behind the lens, and with text on paper, serve rather like shamans to ensure that our culture is recorded and shared so we can flourish.

NANCY ROURKE
Painter

I'd seen Nancy Rourke's artwork online so I figured that readers would be as interested as I was in learning more about her.

Raymond Luczak: Tell us a bit about your background as a Deaf person.

Nancy Rourke: My mother almost lost me when she was pregnant and had to stay in bed through full term. I was born two months premature. However, my parents did not know I was born deaf until I was six years old. The doctor told my parents that I had a learning disability and speech impairment. That was not true. I wore a size 3x5x2-inch box hearing aid wrapped around my chest. I never went to a deaf school. I went to a mainstreamed program from elementary through high school with teachers who knew a little sign. I finally came into the Deaf world at the National Technical Institute for the Deaf (NTID) for the first time in my life. That was where I became more involved in art.

Luczak: What was your childhood like?

Rourke: As a kid, I was always painting and drawing, everything from painting rocks to canvases—had shows at art fairs, in contests, and at galleries at a very young age. I used to bring a big toolbox filled with pens and colored pencils to school everyday. I drew pictures during recesses and exchanged drawings with my deaf friends.

Luczak: What pulled you toward art?

Rourke: My family noticed that I was always drawing and realized it was a way of communicating. They encouraged me to continue with art and that was when I knew what I wanted to be. I studied graphic design and painting at NTID and the Rochester Institute of Technology (RIT) and earned a master's degree in computer graphic design and painting.

Luczak: Who were some of your artist heroes, and why?

Rourke: I am greatly influenced by the Fauvism Movement, the Neo-Expressionist Movement, and the De Stilji Movement—because they used primary colors. I've been told that my paintings seem to be mainly influenced by the American artist Jacob Lawrence (1917-2000). He also used primary colors.

Luczak: Why do you focus on Deaf issues in your work?

Rourke: I have been seeing different sorts of obstacles happening today in the Deaf community, and I feel that my art can provide a message—something to be proud of and to look up to as a Deaf person. More so, through the Deafhood journey.

Luczak: Do you think that hearing people will get it?

Rourke: Yes and no. Some hearing people will get it, and some may take longer to comprehend Deaf art. My paintings are done from a Deaf perspective, and I make the paintings based on how the Deaf see, think, and interact in everyday life. This is a way to grasp hearing people's attention and help them better understand Deaf culture.

Luczak: Do you make your art for Deaf people only?

Rourke: I don't make art for Deaf people only. I make art for those who are Deaf-minded and Deaf-hearted, and for those who are new to the Deaf community. For instance, new parents of Deaf babies and late-deafened adults. I make art for everyone, hearing or Deaf.

Luczak: Tell us a bit about your approach in your work.

Rourke: In my paintings I use primary colors, with a mixture of black and white pigments for saturated color areas. I use these primary colors because to me, that is "Deaf Art Expressionism." Strong brushstrokes make paintings expressive, emotional, and even at times disturbing. I explore issues on Deaf Politics, History, Art, Deaf culture, Linguistics, Audism, and Deafhood.

Luczak: What do you see in Deaf Art and De'VIA? Is there a difference between the two?

Rourke: I see both somewhat similar and somewhat different. Deaf Art can be based on Deaf issues or any subject matter, and the art was created by a Deaf artist. I can visually see "Deaf" in the artwork by Deaf artists, and that is determined by how they use colors, shapes, and styles. Deaf Art is also based on how Deaf artists use their visualization and imagination. Deaf artists gather information much differently than other artists. They rely heavily on their eyes. It is the mind through eyes: a Deaf mind. The eyes pick up details instantly and observe them intensely.

PAMELA E. WITCHER
Artist

A mutual friend from Montreal, Quebec suggested that I look into Pamela's work. I was struck by the wide range of her work.

Raymond Luczak: What do you typically tell a new Deaf person about your background?

Pamela E. Witcher: Hello! *Salut! Bonjour!* I am a versatile artist. I just had my degree in Museology Technology (*Techniques en muséologie* at a French college, 2009 - 2013). I earned a degree in Social Work in 1998, but my art expanded quickly after 2001 when I "saw the light" and decided to adjust my career goals. I also work as a translator and an interpreter between four languages: ASL, LSQ (*Langue des signes québécoise*; also known as Quebec Sign Language), English, and French for 15 years now.

I'm also part of a small company called Groupe BWB. Our goal is to develop and sensitize hearing society about our experiences, our language, our community, and about audism.

Luczak: Were you always a signer?

Witcher: My Deaf parents are from Newfoundland, my second home to Quebec. I have a younger Deaf brother. He now lives with a son of two years old in Ontario. I've always used both ASL and English, with some MSL (Maritime Sign Language). I learned LSQ and French later.

Luczak: Were you encouraged to pursue your artistic interests?

Witcher: During high school, certain people took notice of my graphic, literary, theatrical, and artistic skills. They told me to keep on exploring those areas, to keep on creating. I think it's normal to go through an exploration period between the ages of 20 and 30. After I turned 30 in 2001, I "saw the light," as I've mentioned before, and realized how real an artist I was after the "bang-oh-now-I-see" to the process of my identity build-up and solidification. After I plunged into the art world, I had immense support from the community and my friends. My family has always been present during my various projects. My husband is a wonderful supporter. Artists-colleagues-friends-lovers from the community and other marginal groups are awesome!

Luczak: What kind of media do you tend to work in?

Witcher: I tend to paint with acrylic, sometimes oil, on canvas. Sometimes, I use other mediums such as dry pastel, ink, pencil, and watercolor on paper and canvas. I work with fabric and metal too. I do video editing. I play with languages (ASL, LSQ, IS, English, French, a bit of Latin) in my songs, poems, and stories. I do some graphics and illustrations here and there. I enjoy experimenting with blending everything, with something here and there, and elsewhere.

Luczak: I read "The Phonocentrism Deconstruction Manifesto" on your site, which I've added below. Can you explain what it's about? I'm confused by what "phonocentrism" means.

The ~~Phonocentrism~~ Deconstruction Manifesto focuses on:

1. Reframing from ~~phonocentrism~~ to holistic diversity.
2. Deconstructing logo-~~phonocentric~~ implications in literature, language, image, symbol, behavior, belief, and/or attitude.
3. Works created by linguistic-cultural people of signed languages.
4. Use of any forms of text, such as momentary action, word, painting, drawing, video, digital media, poetry, sculpture, performance, design, installation, calligraphy, film, photography, graphic novel, drama, music, dance, and/or any other forms.
5. Reframing from thought lineage from Plato and Aristotle to thought lineage from the Derrida era.
6. Sculpting language as a malleable material (thought and perception).
7. Advocacy and promotion for language rights of signed languages in both signed and written forms.

Witcher: SPiLL PROpagation organized a workshop with Jolanta Lapiak, a media literary artist who has always been a vivid Jacques Derrida follower. Twelve Canadian artists met for one week for a workshop in four languages (ASL, LSQ, French and English). We communicated by using International Sign with a mix of our native languages here and there. The group had a determination to develop a new manifesto under Jolanta's lead. So *voila*. (The word ~~phonocentrism~~ should have strikethrough, as that's how it's written.) The manifesto was signed at 286 chemin Forgaty, Gatineau, Quebec on May 8, 2014.

The word "phonocentrism" comes from a philosophical view. We had comments from a couple of people from the community disagreeing with the word because of what we have in "ASL phonology," but I had to clarify that we are not portraying a linguistic view. (Please check out SPiLL-PROpagation online for more information.)

A ~~phonocentrism~~ deconstructionist is a creative person who produces a work that questions, challenges and redefines ~~phonocentric~~ construction; seeks to recreate new formation through practice and process; and to induce social change.

Luczak: Your work seems to reveal something of a political awareness as a Deaf activist. Would you agree with that assessment?

Witcher: I have always been an activist. Does my work reveal politics? Hmm. Some of them. They have been viewed as "existentialist" works, as they show the state of being at the present moment and the impact of emotions is direct. Similarly, there are dreamy traits in my work that represent the hopes, dreams, and ideologies of my own and those of the community. Some of my works are community-based, showing the values of attachment to our community and members of/in/around the community. They have also been viewed as De'VIA work.

Luczak: Do you think that there's a difference between art that aims to *educate* as opposed to making a political *statement*? Why or why not?

Witcher: I think there is an overlap between the two different purposes. Art that educates, sensitizes, and spreads awareness is soft and soothing. We adjust, shape, and sing. Art that makes a political statement is hard and provocative. We declare, rebel, and scream. Both of them have the same goal, which is to make ourselves heard, our experiences known.

Both approaches are necessary to create balance, and to make changes, which is why I mentioned the overlap part.

The ~~Phonocentrism~~ Deconstruction workshop has shifted my views in many ways. Right now I need time to digest this approach, and rethink about how my creativity should be shown next.

MARY RAPPAZZO
Painter

When I was looking for potential cover art for one of my new books, I came across Mary Rappazzo's site featuring her stunning artwork.

Raymond Luczak: Could you please tell us a bit about your background growing up? Were you always Deaf?

Mary Rappazzo: I'm a Los Angeles native, growing up in Hollywood and the San Fernando Valley. I have about 70 to 75% loss in both of my ears since birth. Since I was born prematurely at 2.5 pounds, the theory is that my deafness could be related to it. I'm the only one being deaf in my family. For education, my mother was a strong advocate for my mainstream education, including attending a regular public high school.

Sign language was not initially encouraged in the 1960s within the Los Angeles Unified School District. My mother felt that with the help of my hearing aids and residual hearing, I would succeed in the hearing world much further with speech therapy and lipreading than if I relied on signing. It wasn't until in my college years that I started learning sign language and affiliating with the deaf community.

Luczak: How did you become interested in art?

Rappazzo: My grandmother first inspired me to paint representational images such as flowers, old barns, and landscapes, using acrylic medium. I began painting at age ten, with her encouragement, because she felt that I had good spatial ability to create things.

Luczak: Where did you study art?

Rappazzo: Besides my training from my grandmother, I took series of painting classes at Pierce College and California State University at Northridge, where I graduated with a B.A. degree in Graphic Design and a minor in Painting. I was inspired early on by some well-known artists, such as Georgia O'Keeffe and Edward Hopper. I loved their themes and their use of rich colors. I've always been a painter, and also a creative person using a variety of mediums including digital and oil paint.

Luczak: I see that you have a strong preponderance for orange skin, green hair, and one eyes. How did that come about? What do these elements mean to you? Their significance? Do you think they have a bearing on the Deaf experience?

Rappazzo: My painting style is figurative, as it depicts representational images in idealized forms that are not naturalistic. I discovered my signature style in my early 20s: a representation in which I depicted only one eye. The orange skin, green hair, and one-eye elements were developed through my exploration.

In some ways the origins of my paintings are a mystery to me, which is something I love about painting. When I start a painting, I sometimes do not know where or why the image came to me. I don't analyze my inspiration much while I am painting, because I don't want to suppress the creative process. However, when I step back and examine my work, I do see two common themes: One is of people connecting with each other; a second theme that moves me is social justice.

Because my figurative shapes lack emotional definition, the experience of filling in those voids rests with the viewers: The emotions and thoughts that you see in the painting are your own. Perhaps you are reliving your own life experiences, or perhaps you are imagining how you might feel if you were there. I encourage the viewer to let their mind go, to project their emotions and thoughts onto the piece without inhibiting or censoring.

I think my hearing loss enhanced my intuitive abilities, sensitivity, and perceptions of how people engage and interact. Although I don't think about it much on a conscious level, perhaps my experiences as a deaf artist makes me especially attuned to the themes I choose. I have noticed that the figures in my art are often created without a sensory organ or two, yet they are completely engaged in the world around them.

Luczak: Do you see yourself as a Deaf artist? If so, in what way?

Rappazzo: Yes and no: I see myself as an artist, who happens to be Deaf. I don't have a lot of explicit De'VIA in my art, as my art is an expression of the inner self as much as it is a conscious expression of an explicit Deaf imagery like ASL, or I Love You [the ILY handshape]. In my art, there are recurrent themes of people connecting and engaging as well as social justice and injustice that reflects my deafness.

I did several paintings that have explicit deaf imagery, although they don't overpower my subjective themes. For example: one painting called *Embrace* is a child wearing hearing aid and embracing the mother. It is very subtle as the image of hearing aid is only the earpiece with a wire cord. Another painting called *Dinner of Silence* is a retrospective self-portrait about a family dinner in which a little girl has a hearing aid and sitting at the table, but not engaging in the group conversation. Another piece called *Deaf American Gothic* is a more explicit De'VIA image of an old man holding a hearing aid horn instead of a pitchfork. I have experienced pressure as an artist to do more images of deafness. But most of the time I paint what inspires me.

JEREMY QUIROGA
Sculptor and ASL Poet

As part of the first Deaf Artists Residency Program at the Anderson Center for Interdisciplinary Arts in Red Wing, Minnesota, I had the good fortune of getting to know Jeremy better. I was particularly fascinated by his views of art, so we sat down for an interview in ASL, which was translated into English below.

Raymond Luczak: How do you tend to introduce yourself to other people?

Jeremy Quiroga: Lately I've been teasing people by saying that I was born Human and became Human at 20 months old. I went to a Human public school and then graduated from the California School for the Humans. But really—I became deaf at the age of 20 months. I was mainstreamed [in hearing schools] for five years and attended a Deaf residential school for seven years. After High School, I went to Gallaudet University for about one year and then spent the next three years traveling in a VW bus, where I felt the need to see a bit of America. I eventually settled down in Seattle, Washington, but my wife and I decided it was time for me to go back to school. We moved to Rochester, New York, where I earned a B.F.A. and M.F.A. in Metal Sculpture from the Rochester Institute of Technology (RIT). The graduate degree gave me the experience to teach metal sculpture and I was the first Deaf person to teach an elective art class at RIT. In my first year as a graduate student, I had to observe how the class was taught, and then in my second year, I taught the class. The first thing I always told my students—didn't matter if they were hearing or Deaf—that just like they were students from different cultures like Korean and Chinese, art was also a language but without words. We looked at art as a language and discussed that from many perspectives.

Luczak: How has the meaning of art evolved for you over the years?

Quiroga: The title of my graduate thesis was *Deaf Cuban American Male Makes Art*. I was being sarcastic, but a variety of factors did influence me as a person and therefore my work.

Sometimes certain expectations are imposed on Deaf artists from within the community. If an artist is Deaf, they are expected to create De'VIA work. This creates unnecessary pressure to create art just to fit within those parameters.

I've found this to be really awkward for me. I've had a big misunderstanding with some of these people who expect Deaf artists to subscribe to the De'VIA movement, and only because I've said that I'm not De'VIA! I was just stating a fact about my work. I have made over 100 pieces of art, two out of which could be considered De'VIA. My own Deaf experience would be conveyed in these two pieces. Of course, if I had made 90 pieces that focused on my Deaf experience, I'd call myself a De'VIA artist. De'VIA has been clearly defined, and my work doesn't fit their definition.

Luczak: So when you create art, you don't think in terms of labels?

Quiroga: Yes, that's right. I'd like to see a new direction in art that focuses on celebrating ASL. I could be wrong in how I view De'VIA, but my overall impression is that De'VIA art focuses solely on the emotional aspects of being Deaf: frustrations, oppression, expression, rebellion, demands, communal strength.

Luczak: Would you consider them negative emotions?

Quiroga: Not necessarily. Those are important. Of course, if you analyze being Deaf or being oppressed, it can look negative. If you interact with a gay person [about his background], you can find oppression there. If you interact with a black person, you'll also find oppression there. I don't see that as a negative thing; just reality. It's just that I find the Deaf label too restrictive. If you're Deaf, they will run a checklist against you to see if you fit in with their expectations. For example, with my ASL poetry, one can say that it has a lot more to do with the Deaf experience than my own sculpture. Yet within the De'VIA parameters, ASL poetry has no place there. Why is that? That shows how restrictive De'VIA is.

As a Deaf person, I was deeply inspired by De'VIA. It's very important, like [Susan Dupor's painting] *Family Dog*; that painting truly affected me. Chuck Baird's art touched me too. I found Ann Silver's work to be awesome even though it is a Pop Art style. And there were many others. Let's look at what's happened with black art: First, there was rage and rebellion, but it eventually shifted into a celebratory mode. There are Deaf artists out there who acknowledge the importance of De'VIA, but they want to focus on celebrating Sign. They see Sign in a very positive way. As a Human, if I were to analyze every little thing that has oppressed me all my life, I would feel "eaten up" with all those turbulent emotions pushing about inside me. I'd like to put those aside and look at the illuminations of Sign. Celebrate Sign like how George Veditz did: He saw Sign as a gift. Celebrating Sign should be more inclusive so that it's not just Deaf people sharing their experiences. I know that some Deaf people will bristle at my suggestion—"ASL is ours!"—but what about CODAs and other hearing people who've become immersed in our signing community? Rejecting those people is . . . well, I'm not sure if that's right. Again, I think it's important to celebrate ASL and inspire the people who use it.

It was important to go through that period of rage and rebellion, but is it worth sustaining forever? We are asking for a burnout right there. We would run out of energy from fighting so much. Statistically speaking, ASL is the third most popular foreign language to learn in America. This doesn't mean that oppression of Deaf people has gone away; just like it hasn't for gay people or black people. I'd agree, though, that we are in a better place in a lot of ways.

Luczak: You told me a new theory of yours. Could you expound on it?

Quiroga: After being involved with the Deaf Artists Residency program for a month here, I've been doing a lot of thinking and discussing with others about this. I'd like to call this movement ASLism, just like Surrealism, Realism, and other art movements. Again, this is my own opinion: De'VIA has become a box. Of course, all labels are boxes, but with De'VIA, I feel it's run its course. It's stuck with no room for growth. For example, you can't put ASL poetry into that box, so where else can ASL poetry go? That's why I want to look at the idea of celebrating Sign.

Another example: I was watching how Lilah Katcher, a Deaf poet here, worked. It was fascinating to see how ASL influenced her writing. But her work wouldn't be accepted as part of De'VIA simply because it was in English. Which is silly, because ASL inspired her, and it goes back to my original point: We should celebrate ASL itself. Stories written in ASL gloss would be another example that would be rejected only because English was used.

I feel it's time for a new label, or look for something beyond De'VIA. Two years ago I suggested to everyone a simple concept: "Post-De'VIA." A number of artists got upset. I was disappointed by that reaction. But no one can stay the same forever. Labels are important, but we need to move on. New generation, new thinking, new inspirations. Art movements tend to last a specific period, ranging from ten to maybe 30 years.

I have no specific ideas how ASLism should be defined. It's still a very new concept for me, but people should discuss it with each other and see what transpires. All I know is that it should celebrate ASL as a language.

Luczak: Basically you're saying that if anything—regardless of form or medium—is influenced by ASL or uses ASL in some way, it would be considered part of ASLism?

Quiroga: Yes. One possible approach to use in ASLism is "WHALE," the sculpture I'm working on right now. It's very realistic, from the whale's head smashing into the waves, but its tail is the same as the ASL handshape for "WHALE." Its movement going into the waves is the same movement used in the ASL sign for "WHALE." That sculpture uses realism yet celebrates ASL at the same time. It's inspired by Chuck Baird's work where he combined both sign and imagery in the same painting.

Luczak: Any words of advice for young Deaf artists?

Quiroga: Don't be afraid. No matter what people may think or say, stay true to your own feelings. If it feels right, do it.

ADREAN CLARK
Artist

Adrean Clark is one of those people who seems to be in a constant state of evolution. I'd known her when she and her husband John Lee Clark ran The Tactile Mind Press back in the early 2000s.

Raymond Luczak: Can you share something about your background as a Deaf person?

Adrean Clark: I was born into a hearing family and most of my childhood was spent in a mainstreamed environment. When I transferred to the Central North Carolina School for the Deaf (CNCSD) in eighth grade, it changed for the better how I perceived myself as a deaf person. Being immersed in a fully accessible ASL environment at the school was wonderful. I was able to focus on being a person without being reminded of having "broken ears."

Luczak: Were you always interested in art?

Clark: I've always been interested in expressing myself in different creative ways. It's more about communicating an idea rather than how it's communicated. I wrote poetry and short humor until I realized cartoons and comic strips would convey my ideas better. One of my first poems appeared in *Good Apple* magazine.

Luczak: What pulled you into drawing cartoons?

Clark: Some of my early memories at CNCSD was drawing cartoon dragons for other students. It was difficult in the beginning because I had been raised with Signing Exact English (SEE) and was thrown right into the ASL environment without any classes. Art was one way to connect with others and build friendships.

I have finished seven books so far, of which five are illustrated. My comic strips, *Deaf Profiles* and *My Hands Full*, ran for several years in *SIGNews*. I've learned that creating a book is like giving birth to children—it's a lot of work, and you have to take care of the contents all the way to the finish line. It takes me longer to finish a book than it does shorter projects but the end result is immensely satisfying.

Luczak: I've noticed that you often write in ASL. Has that helped you in your work as an artist?

Clark: The thing about written ASL is that it helps one see the inner workings of ASL. My deaf school experience was wonderful but I wasn't given any ASL classes or training that would help me express myself better. When I started writing, things finally began to make sense and I could identify the elements to ASL that would help with comprehension.

Writing ASL also helped me see how much English limits ASL. John and I had already explored the concept of a signing community through The Tactile Mind Press, so over time the concept became even more personal. Now I consider myself more as an culturally ASL person rather than "deaf."

Think of it this way—the word "Deaf" literally means that we are accepting the label of "broken ears" that hearing people gave us and being proud of it. When we're signing in ASL there's no such thing as "broken ears"—there's only communication through the hands. There should be a new ASL word for our identity as primary ASL communicators instead of the English glossed "Deaf."

The overall process supercharged my creativity as an artist. I can see things now that not everyone sees, so my current work has a lot to do with making tangible what was previously impossible to imagine.

Luczak: It appears that you're no longer limited to paper as a means of expression, and that one of your artworks appeared on a T-shirt.

Clark: The first time I published a book, it was amazing. I spent a large amount of my childhood with my nose in a book, and to take on the identity of an author with a finished product in my hands . . . It was (and still is) a great feeling. I didn't want to stop there.

My vision is for ASL to be as much a part of our country as English. That means not only in books but in the world around us. I want to see a broad spectrum of ASL materials from the artistic to the mundane. Instead of waiting for it to happen, my sleeves are rolled up and my hands are making those things. Hopefully others will join in!

Luczak: Some Deaf artists feel that the De'VIA label is too restrictive. Do you feel that way?

Clark: Why would those artists feel that way? It's only a label for a little part of the big art world. If there were more art historians studying deaf artists, they'd probably see a lot more going on than just De'VIA.

Sometimes because we feel so small because of oppression, we try to stretch the few labels we have to fit everything. We might even spend time waiting for English labels rather than inventing new ASL ones! I can see how De'VIA might feel restricting—but really, the intention of the movement name is to name something that is already happening, rather than categorize something for artists to fit in.

My feeling is that the next art movement within our community will be centered around an ASL identity. What it will be called or how it will happen, I don't know—but the signs of it happening are already there.

Luczak: Some years ago you called yourself a cartoonist. Do you still call yourself that, or is there a new label you've come to prefer?

Clark: I don't consider myself a cartoonist anymore, because the work I've produced has since been on a broad spectrum. What's important to me is communicating the idea—how it's expressed depends on what fits it the best. I consider myself an artist, until a better name comes along.

Luczak: What sort of things do you foresee yourself doing five, ten years from now?

Clark: Hopefully I'll be reading your written ASL novel, Raymond!

It's hard to look ahead to the future as I'm already working on it now. The rest depends on the ASL community.

MATTHEW JENKINS
Painter

When I learned of a British Deaf artist who used house paint in his paintings, I was a bit surprised. House paint? I had to find out more.

Raymond Luczak: Tell us about your background as a Deaf person. How were you educated?

Matthew Jenkins: My father was hammering on the wall one day while my mother helped him to straighten the frame hung on the wall and then they realized that I had to be deaf when they saw me sleeping in her arm. I grew up in a Deaf family since my parents and sister are all Deaf. My father was anti-mainstream, so that was how my parents had refused to let their children to be educated in a local mainstream school with its low educational standards. My father decided to fight for better education for us. My father placed my Deaf sister to the grammar school for the deaf in Newbury, England. He encouraged me to follow in her footstep to the grammar school. After I failed to get into my sister's grammar school as I hadn't realized that it was an oral school for the deaf. I was placed in my father's boarding school in the deep heart of Surrey on the outskirt belt of Greater London; I stayed there until the school closed. Then I went to boarding school in the famous "chalk" coast of southeast England. I returned to Wales after leaving school and went to a local college to study art as that was always my path since I won a painting competition when I was four years old. I gained two degrees in two different universities in Wolverhampton (BA Hons) and Cardiff (MA); I'm considering doing a Ph.D. in Deaf Arts at Bristol University this fall.

Luczak: How did you become interested in art?

Jenkins: My hometown where my family grew up was actually a part of how I became an artist. We lived in a squashed seaside town that had two different aspects at the end of my street—a mountain and steel factories. On one side you could see many details and surfaces on the mountain; on the other side you could see smoke coming out of the factories. It was almost like surrealism, where the smoke flew up in all sorts of shapes and how it joined the clouds. My father is a graphic designer, and my mother was a sewing machinist. They have been and were always my role models, which inspired my elder sister and me to study for art degrees.

Luczak: It appears that you use house paint for your artwork. Isn't that odd?

Jenkins: No, it is not odd. People often said, "You should not allowed to use house paint. It's not art. It must be painted with oil." I wondered, "Who said I was not allowed?" It was like being told not to sign. I realized that I needed to stand up for myself and believe in myself. University lecturers saw it in me, and they encouraged me to use more house paint. I realized that I could create beautiful pieces of art. Remember that in the past, when traditional artists first saw the work of Impressionist painters, they rejected those. Suddenly these "rejected" artists were hung proudly in the major art galleries. Change in art is sometimes good. If we don't let Deaf art change, there is no story left to tell.

Luczak: Where do you think that Deaf artists will go in the future?

Jenkins: They should open like a flower within themselves and go mainstream. They shouldn't sit there, waiting for someone to help them with prospects; it won't happen. Being artists, they have to rely on themselves. They need to stand up for themselves, and seek out the highest mountains, climb up on them, and grab the shining star above themselves. They need to believe in it, and everyone will be able to recognize their work as a true artist. They are the only ones who can build their future as artists.

CYNTHIA WEITZEL
Arts Administrator and Artist

I remember the exact date when I first met Cynthia Weitzel: July 19, 1984. It was our first day of the New Signers Program at Gallaudet University, and we were both freshmen. Thirty years later our paths happily converged again.

Raymond Luczak: What were your growing up years like?

Cynthia Weitzel: For years, whenever people would ask me to explain what my childhood was like, my first response would be, "It's complicated." Deaf friends had often assumed I had it easy because I grew up in a home with Deaf parents. Or hearing friends thought it must have been so tough growing up with Deaf parents. Truth is, it was neither tough nor easy, but it was complicated.

Because I started out hard of hearing, my parents decided to first try me out in the local hearing schools. Then if, and when, it became too much of a struggle, they would transfer me to the school for the deaf, either to St. John's in Milwaukee or Wisconsin School for the Deaf in Delevan. I was the only kid in school who was either hard of hearing or deaf, and there were no interpreters or support back then, especially not in small rural towns like ours.

Most of my learning was through lipreading, usually bits and pieces when not daydreaming, or through textbooks after hours. School days were painfully boring and even more painfully long. I was Deaf by the time I was in middle school and by then already well on my way to becoming a functioning alcoholic. The parents of one of my close friends owned a liquor store in town so access to booze was easy. Vodka became my best friend and vice for surviving the stress and boredom of school. I kept my school struggles quiet from my parents for fear they would send me away. I wanted nothing more than to be at a Deaf school, but it would mean leaving my family and my liquor source—something that I wasn't willing to do at the time. As long as I kept up my grades, I was able to keep up the charade. I was a good observer and able to quickly adapt to just about any situation. My mantra then was "Fake it until you make it," and that meant anything and everything to act as if I knew what was going on. Code-switching was a daily routine—hearing norms while in school, Deaf norms while at home.

Luczak: What have you learned from your time at Gallaudet?

Weitzel: Growing up, my family was mostly engaged in sports and the outdoors, but at Gallaudet, I was exposed to the visual arts, theater, and dance performed by or from the perspective of Deaf artists. I had no prior awareness, knowledge or understanding of Deaf arts, or that it even existed.

At Gallaudet, I remember how exciting and enjoyable it was to sit back and relax while watching a lecture or discussion in my natural language. I became a sponge, and for the first time school was no longer something I dreaded—I was in love with learning. Unfortunately, I also fell in love with the social scene and D.C. nightlife. Like a moth to a flame, I could not get enough. Eventually my nightlife took precedence over my academic life. I don't think I attended even one class during the spring semester; I was just living there. By the end of that first year I was politely asked to leave, and so I did. I was very disappointed in myself for allowing that to happen. I had wanted nothing more than to continue on and graduate with my Class of '88, but looking back, I have no regrets. I needed to break out of my shell in a big way, and I did just that. When I left, I headed south to stay with a friend for the summer so I could drink and get high in peace. From then on, I stayed underground for the next couple years until I hit my bottom and sought help via 12-Step Recovery. I've been sober and clean since 1987.

Luczak: We reconnected in 2007 when you began working at the State Capitol in St. Paul. What was that like?

Weitzel: I had just moved back to Minnesota after my husband and I lived out of state for a number of years. By this time, I had more than 20 years of experience under my belt in the nonprofit field. But I had no direct experience in public policy. When I was offered the position of public policy coordinator and lobbyist by the Commission of Deaf, DeafBlind & Hard of Hearing Minnesotans, I was up for the challenge but had no idea what a steep learning curve this would be for me. I had jumped in midway through legislative session during a record-breaking year of passing eight new pieces of legislation while also supporting four others—three to four times more than what the Commission normally has on its agenda for any given session. To say that it was "baptism by fire" would be an understatement! At the same time, it was thrilling to be actively engaged in this process and a part of this history.

I stayed with the Commission for a few years, and I gained so much knowledge, experience and insight into the process of effecting change through policy. I had been previously accustomed to seeing changes in people by one person at a time—wonderful but often short-lived while systems remained the same. After joining the Commission, it was all about systems change for long-term impact improving lives and opportunity for our entire community.

I also learned the value of community organizing. Protesting and calling attention to issues is only half the equation to effecting change. Many avid protesters of years past are now engaged with the legislative process because they realized public opinion alone would not actively change systems. The decisionmakers who represent the masses are the ones who ultimately carry out the policy changes necessary to effect change. Influence the decisionmakers (or become a decisionmaker), and you'll see change.

Luczak: Have you always been an artist?

Weitzel: I can't remember a time when I wasn't drawn to the arts, especially the visual arts. As a child, when not in school, I spent most of my time outdoors exploring the wonders and beauty in nature. We lived on a swollen lake area of the river with protected forest and wetlands across the way and upriver with the dam downriver. Like a young female Huck Finn always in search of adventure, the river was a place of freedom for me from the restrictive *sivilizing* or assimilation within the all-hearing school and town. It was a living art gallery, haven, and playground all in one. This was one place where I could simply be me.

Once I was older and formal art classes were introduced to the schedule, it was always then that they would schedule me instead for speech therapy so as not to pull me out of the more important academic classes. After spending so much time in the basement "learning my lesson," I stopped speaking up about it and just went along with the flow. No art classes for me. But by high school I was so desperate to leave that I loaded my schedule with every additional advanced class I could to ensure my odds for obtaining a college scholarship to Gallaudet—my ticket to freedom. Once again, I let art classes pass me by. This isn't to say that I wasn't artistic and creative in all that I did because I was, but with no formal training.

I never forgot my first encounter with Deaf arts. I had returned to Gallaudet in the summer of 1989 for the Deaf Way International Festival—it was mind-blowing! Being immersed within Deaf visual, literary, and performing arts as well as Deaf history all that week was life-altering. Never had I experienced anything so eye-opening and affirming. I knew then and there that this is what fueled my deepest passions. I knew that someday this would be the direction I would take for myself.

Later, at a Deaf Studies conference in Chicago where I saw Deborah Blumenson give a lecture about Deaf artists and the still-nascent De'VIA movement, it became clear how these works visually described our common shared experiences that I had always struggled to put into words. Who among us in the Deaf community hasn't stopped dead in our tracks when first witnessing *Ameslan Prohibited* by Betty G. Miller, *Family Dog* by Susan Dupor, *Crying Hands* by David Bloch, *Milan, Italy 1880* by Mary Thornley, or *We, the Deaf People* by Chuck Baird? These works and others were fostering dialogue concerning topics that not too long before were still taboo or topics often only broached in academia.

Earlier, in my freshman year at Gallaudet, I was first exposed to elements of Deaf history beyond my parents' storytelling, which gave me a sense of having roots. I've always been a very curious person, so when I wasn't out all night exploring D.C., I could be found burrowed deep in the Gallaudet Archives. I was in awe. I was inspired. And I eventually was hooked on history. The more I learned about our history, the more proud and confident I became as a Deaf woman.

Access to art history has been both inspiring and educational. The same is true about Deaf history only at a level much more personal. Deaf history, including Deaf art history, has helped to make clear the many emotions I harbored for years but didn't always know why or how to describe. Or things I've always known to be true about our language, culture and shared experiences as Deaf people but didn't have the background of which to best explain it to others. The saying "Know your history, know yourself" could not be more true. As an artist and activist, I can't imagine being able to move forward without knowing where it is I came from—physically, spiritually, emotionally, psychologically, and politically. History matters, art matters, we matter. It's all relevant.

But it wasn't until I was 30 that I returned to college a third time, this time to obtain my degree in business management. This was while we were living in middle Tennessee. I attended Austin Peay State University in Clarksville, and they provided a team of top-notch ASL interpreters for all my classes. That was when I signed up for my first formal art class. By this time I had put in eight years as an alcohol and drug counselor and program coordinator in Minnesota and Tennessee, and I was needing to feed my own soul and recovery again. In those days there were only a handful of Deaf Alcohol and Drug Abuse counselors, including the artist Betty G. Miller whom I knew first as colleague then later as fellow artist; also, services were limited so we were commonly stretched very thin, and the burnout rate was very high. I was not immune to this, and I knew danger was ahead for my own recovery if I didn't take a timeout or act to bring better balance into my life, so I did both.

At first my intention was to simply take a few art classes to gain skill in being able to explore visual arts in my own free time when not working. Halfway through my first week of art classes my intention changed. I realized this needed to be more than a hobby and something I would eventually do as a career, so I added Fine Art as a second major. For the next five years, full-time year-round, I bounced back and forth between the schools of arts and business—nonstop right-brain and left-brain aerobics—and I was in heaven. I took more courses than what was required for my BFA, especially in Art History, but I didn't have time to complete a show and internship before needing to return to work, so in December 2000 I received my BBA-Business Management with a Minor in Fine Art Studio.

After another ten years in the nonprofit field, I finally had the opportunity to consider transitioning out of the nonprofit field and into a career as professional artist. Following a long mystery illness which affected my memory, balance, vision, and host of other things, I was at a crossroads. After many months of testing and slow recovery, the Mayo Clinic diagnosed me with having chronic fatigue syndrome and chronic vestibular migraines brought on by a lifetime of undetected and untreated congenital defects since birth. The Treacher Collins Syndrome was obvious, same as my mother's, so no surprise there, but issues affecting my vertebral arteries, thymus, and stomach had been simply overlooked. Aging and a long history of overworking suddenly brought my body to a screeching halt. I will never be back to my normal, but with significant diet and lifestyle changes, I'm able to better manage it.

While figuring out what I was going to do for the rest of my life, I rented studio space for a nominal fee during the cold winter months at the Anderson Center at Tower View. It was a place to simply get out of the house and create whenever I felt up to it. This was very therapeutic and motivated me to work all that much harder at getting my health back in shape.

When spring rolled around and it was time for me to move out of my temporary studio space, I asked if there were other options for temporary studio space at the Anderson Center (AC). Its director, Robert Hedin, asked instead if I would like to stay on as a permanent year-round resident. They do have a waiting list, but decisions are based on wanting to make sure there is balance and diversity within the community of artists and not all of the same focus, style or discipline. They said if I accepted, I would be given the "chicken coop." I gladly accepted. At this time the chicken coop was in very rough, rundown shape and undergoing renovation which I thought was going to be minor; simple cleaning and repairs, enough to make it habitable. Once it was completed, though, I was stunned to find myself moving into one of the most beautiful studio spaces on campus—a diamond in the rough now shining brilliantly. How did I ever get so lucky? This new lifestyle works out beautifully in that it is flexible and close to home so that I can simply work around my health while doing what I love most. I could not ask for a better solution.

Luczak: What led you to pursue the idea of setting up a new Deaf Artist Residency program there?

Weitzel: After being welcomed into the AC community in 2011, it didn't take me long to realize the value and benefits of interaction with other resident artists. I was curious to find out just how many residency programs in this country, and abroad, were considered "Deaf-friendly" either by making themselves accessible via ASL interpreters or by hosting groups of Deaf artists at a time. I can't say I was surprised to learn of only one artist residency program in the world considered to be Deaf-friendly and that is Siena Art Institute's Summer Residency Program. The building and campus was originally home to Siena's Institute for the Deaf (*ToIstituto Pendola*). And today the National Deaf Association (*Ente Nazionale Sordi*) still occupies the ground floor.

According to the Alliance for Artist Communities, there are roughly 500 residency programs in the U.S. while internationally there are over 1,500. Honestly, I was shocked at the number. I rarely heard of Deaf artists applying or being accepted into residency programs, and those artists who did engage in artist-in-residence programs tended to do so at schools for the deaf where communication was direct and fluid instead of through interpreters. Also, in this scenario, the artists are usually doing all the giving and not receiving or benefiting from artistic/cultural exchanges among fellow artists.

As my relationship with AC grew, the idea of hosting a culturally-based Deaf Artist Residency Program (DARP) for established and emerging artists whose natural or adoptive language was ASL evolved. During the winter of 2013, I formally pitched the idea to Robert Hedin. The idea was well received and after getting approval from the board, we submitted our proposal to the National Endowment for the Arts (NEA) that spring for funding to underwrite the pilot program. In November 2013 we received word from NEA of our proposal being accepted. We couldn't have been more pleased and acted immediately to put out the call to artists about this opportunity.

The number of applications submitted by Deaf artists was right on par with the average number of applications received by artists in general for each of the other months open to artists visiting from May to October of each year. But it took much doing to get the word out since this was a new, unfamiliar opportunity within our community. We don't have a strong point of reference as to what residency programs are all about, let alone experience in putting together a strong application and work plan for this type of offering. Many hours were spent on answering questions and educating interested applicants about the process. But it was all worth it!

Prior to the start of DARP, the Anderson Center was hesitant to committing to any long-range plans about this becoming an ongoing program. Then just one week after the arrival of the five Deaf artists in June 2014, AC has committed to offering DARP at least every two years, depending on funding.

It was just as much a learning experience for AC as it was for the five Deaf artists-in-residence. Robert Hedin himself has said, "In the Anderson Center's twenty-plus year history of hosting more than 700 visiting artists in residence from all over the world, this group of residents having participated in the Deaf Artists Residency Program is by far one of the finest groups we've ever had in terms of talent, professionalism, and cohesiveness."

Luczak: Now that you've finished its first year, what have you learned from the entire process? What should other artist residency programs be aware of if they decide to establish something similar?

Weitzel: I'd have to say what I learned most about this entire process is that it was worth every ounce of energy invested into making this happen. We are sincerely indebted to these five artists participating in the first DARP for their patience and contributions while this was a pilot program and one being well-documented through photos, film and the media. They were also incredibly generous with their time and talents by participating in three community service events as opposed to the usual one or two to ensure the program's success.

The outcome of this first-time experience exceeded all expectations, so much that Alliance for Artist Communities (AAC) has invited me as a representative of AC to join a panel presentation made up of speakers from NEA (its accessibility division), Vermont Residency Center (the largest in America), and 3Arts (a Chicago-based nonprofit grantmaking organization focused on artists of underserved populations) during the annual AAC conference to share solutions for making residency opportunities more accessible and meaningful from a "holistic point-of-view" as opposed to traditional means.

It is our hope that other residency programs will follow this example and offer similar opportunities from this holistic cultural approach in their respective areas so that Deaf artists, like other artists, will one day have a range of opportunities to choose from for residencies. And since not all residency programs are alike, it would be in everyone's best interest to work in partnership with local Deaf artists or Deaf arts organizations while considering the development of these new opportunities. Such partnerships would be vital for training of staff and residency review panel in advance of the program being launched. Of course, it goes without saying that a qualified member of the Deaf arts community should always be included in the residency review panel. AC will likely develop a guide sheet or booklet offering suggestions for best practices concerning the above until a national Deaf arts guild is established to take on this task within the scope of its work.

Eventually, as more and more Deaf friendly residency opportunities become available, we're going to see the field of Deaf arts grow in talent and become even more vibrant, just as we've all witnessed in other communities of minority or diasporan artists. I'm confident this will be happening sooner than later, thanks to all Deaf artists before us who have laid the initial foundation upon which this work will be built.

RAYMOND LUCZAK
Author and Editor

Born and raised as the only one deaf in a family of nine children in Michigan's Upper Peninsula, Raymond Luczak lost much of his hearing at the age of eight months due to a bout of double pneumonia and high fever, but this was not detected until he was two and a half years old. From that point on, he wore hearing aids and learned to speak. He was not allowed to use sign language until he was 14. After graduating from Houghton High School in 1984, Luczak moved to Washington, D.C. to attend Gallaudet University, the world's only liberal arts university for the Deaf. After participating in the Deaf President Now movement with his Class of '88, he graduated with a B.A. in English. A few months later he moved to New York City where he would live for the next 17 years. He soon scored a national breakthrough with his essay "Notes of a Deaf Gay Writer" on the cover of *Christopher Street* magazine. A few years later his first book, *Eyes of Desire: A Deaf Gay & Lesbian Reader*, won two Lambda Literary Award nominations. His work has been nominated three times for the Pushcart Prize.

Since then Luczak has gone on to write and edit 15 more books, including the novel *Men with Their Hands,* which won first place in the Project: QueerLit 2006 Contest, and *How to Kill Poetry*. He is the editor of *Jonathan*, a fiction journal featuring the work of queer male writers. He is also a playwright and filmmaker.

In 2005, he moved to Minneapolis, Minnesota where he is constantly trying out new recipes while his terrier mix Rocky proves to be an excellent sniffer in the kitchen. He can be found online at raymondluczak.com.